ALGEBRA OUT LOUD

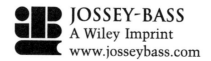

Learning Mathematics Through Reading and Writing Activities

PAT MOWER

JOSSEY-BASS
A Wiley Imprint
www.josseybass.com

Published by Jossey-Bass
A Wiley Imprint
989 Market Street, San Francisco, CA 94103-1741   www.josseybass.com

Jossey-Bass books and products are available through most bookstores. To contact Jossey-Bass directly call our Customer Care Department within the U.S. at 800-956-7739, outside the U.S. at 317-572-3986 or fax 317-572-4002.

Jossey-Bass also publishes its books in a variety of electronic formats. Some content that appears in print may not be available in electronic books.

ISBN 0–7879–6898–6

Printed in the United States of America
FIRST EDITION
PB Printing   10 9 8 7 6 5 4 3

The Author

Pat Mower is an associate professor in the Department of Mathematics and Statistics, Washburn University, in Topeka, Kansas. She earned a B.S. with a double major in mathematics and English from Dickinson State University in North Dakota, an M.S. in mathematics with a minor in statistics, and a Ph.D. in teacher education with specialization in mathematics education at the University of North Dakota. Currently, she prepares preservice teachers to teach mathematics in elementary, middle, and secondary schools. Her interests include reading and writing in mathematics, alternative methods regarding the teaching and learning of mathematics, and basset hounds.

Acknowledgments

I could not have written this book without the assistance and support of my editor, Steve Thompson; the love and encouragement of my husband and my hero, Derek; the suggestions and editing from my wonderful mother, Kathy; and the doggy hugs from my bassets, Samantha and Sadie Sue.

Contents

Introduction

Algebra Out Loud introduces selected reading and writing strategies and activities that are appropriate for algebra courses at the secondary and college levels. The first step in learning to communicate mathematics effectively is understanding the mathematics, and the first step to understanding mathematics is learning to read mathematics effectively. Borasi and Siegal (1990) suggest that the key components for reading to learn mathematics are a rich variety of math texts, transactional reading strategies, and a compatible curricular framework. Another key component in understanding mathematics is being able to communicate the understanding through the written word.

Algebra Out Loud presents several classroom-tested reading strategies and activities. Many of the reading strategies presented come directly from the curricula of Reading in the Content Area courses and texts such as *Teaching Reading in the Content Areas* (Billmeyer and Barton, 1998), and many of the writing strategies and activities come from the curricula of writing courses. I have selected only the strategies from these courses that support mathematical learning. Other strategies and activities in this book come directly from my experiences in the mathematics classroom and address the uniqueness of algebraic text and of writing about algebra. These activities focus on areas such as reading, writing, and understanding applications (word problems), proofs, algebraic concepts, and the algebraic learning process. This book is divided into two parts: "Reading to Learn Algebra" and "Writing to Learn Algebra."

Over the years, I have found that algebra students often do not read the text or merely use the text for reference. Many times, I have heard students say something like the following: "I get it when I see it on the board, but I do not understand the text." The goal of this book is to help students understand mathematical text by giving teachers examples and lessons to be used in the classroom that promote effective and efficient reading habits. "Reading to Learn Algebra" includes strategies and activities for prior to, during, and after the reading of text. I suggest choosing texts and supplementary readings that are reader-friendly, although more often than not this is a judgment call.

Part One contains four chapters. Chapter One, "Prereading Strategies and Activities," presents reading strategies, activities, and ideas that activate students' prior knowledge, prepare and motivate the students to read mathematical content, and guide students in previewing activities. Each strategy or activity is presented in a WHAT? (a description), WHY? (objectives), and HOW? (examples or lessons) format.

Chapter Two, "Reading and Vocabulary-Building Strategies and Activities," focuses on effective and efficient reading strategies, activities, and ideas to be used by the student during the reading process. This chapter includes vocabulary-building activities that enlarge and enhance the mathematical vocabulary of the mathematics student.

Chapter Three, "Postreading Strategies and Activities," presents reading strategies, activities, and ideas that assist the mathematics student in summarizing, analyzing, presenting, using, and retaining mathematical content. Several lessons address study habits.

Chapter Four, "Readings in Algebra," contains four extra lessons and/or readings in mathematics created specifically for this book. Several examples and lessons in earlier chapters refer to these readings.

Part Two of this book, "Writing to Learn Algebra," addresses four areas in writing about algebra. All of the writing strategies and activities, the majority of which are from experiences in my classrooms, are centered about the algebra curriculum.

Chapter Five, "Writing to Understand Algebra," presents writing strategies and activities that ask students to write about algebraic vocabulary, processes, theorems, definitions, and graphs. These activities are usually handed in to the teacher to be assessed. Several lessons are included in this chapter.

Chapter Six, "Writing to Communicate Algebra," presents activities that focus on communicating mathematical ideas to peers and to the teacher. These writings may or may not be graded.

Chapter Seven, "Writing as Authentic Assessment," presents activities that are usually ungraded and become a part of personal assessment for the student.

Chapter Eight, "Writing for Assessment," presents activities where students write about algebra as part of their graded work.

The References cite the work used to compile and create these strategies, activities, and ideas.

As you use the ideas presented in this book and create your own lessons, I wish for you the same delight and satisfaction of being part of a community of students actively engaged in the communicating and learning of mathematics that I have encountered.

Algebra Time Line

3000–1000 B.C.

First algebraic ideas emerge: Egyptians write hieroglyphic numbers. General ideas behind linear equations written on Rhind and moscow papyri.

Babylonians use cuneiform numbers. Pythagorean theorem, quadratic equations, and systems of equations written on clay tablets.

1000 B.C.–0

Indians develop square root calculations and use the Pythagorean theorem.

Greeks prove algebraic ideas using a straight edge and a compass.

Chinese explore square and cube roots and systems of linear equations.

0–800 A.D.

Diophantus (Egypt) used number theory to solve indeterminate equations.

Development of the Hindu-Arabic decimal place value number system.

800–1000

Algebraic techniques developed in India.

Al-Khwárizmi invents the algorithm and writes the first algebra text. The term *algebra* is derived from *al-jabr,* meaning reunion and reduction, also applied to bonesetting. Algebra is mostly rhetorical.

1000–1400

The beginnings of a search for general algebraic symbols: Leonardo Fibonacci invents a new symbolism called syncopated algebra, a very complex form of symbolism.

The Chinese invent Chinese remainder theorem, explore Pascal's triangle, and solve polynomial equations.

1400–1600

Girolamo Cardan publishes Nicolo Tartaglia's solution for solving cubic equations, causing a huge scandal. François Viete develops algebraic symbolism, with vowels for unknowns and consonants for constants.

1600–1700

René Descartes develops the Cartesian coordinate system. Sir Isaac Newton and Gottfried Leibniz vie for status of the "inventor" or discoverer of calculus.

1700–1800

Leonhard Euler invents symbols like *"f(x),"* making algebra simpler to read and write.

1800–1900

Algebraic number theory.

David Hilbert poses twenty-three unsolved equations and proofs for the next era of mathematicians to solve.

1900–2000

Computers and calculators change the teaching of algebra, as well as the world. Wiles proves Fermat's theorem in 1993.

National Council of Teachers of Mathematics presents standards for mathematical instruction and encourages algebraic concepts to be taught in the elementary grades, as well as in the middle and high school grades.

Part One

Reading to Learn Algebra

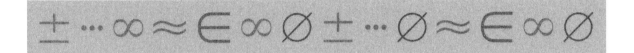

That Language is an instrument of human reason, and not merely a medium for the expression of thought, is a truth generally admitted.

George Boole, 1854

$\pm \cdots \infty \approx \in \infty \varnothing \pm \cdots \varnothing \approx \in \infty \varnothing$

Prereading Strategies and Activities

Prelude

Mathematics students will readily admit they often skip over the mathematical text and go right to the problem section of a lesson in the text. As teachers, we attempt to remedy the situation by cajoling and coaxing the students to open the book and read. However, we suspect that many of our students pay little attention to this, for they know that they will learn the important content from our presentation of the content in class or can refer back to examples in the text for help with assigned problems. What appears to be missing is the students' willingness to read and learn from the text. So if willingness is the key, how do we instill this in our students?

We know that children learn to read after they have demonstrated a readiness to learn. We can surmise that when our students are ready to read mathematical text, they will do so. So our role seems clear: facilitate this readiness. The key components for readiness to learn are interest, competence, and confidence. First, the text must capture the attention of the reader by containing content that is both interesting and relevant. Also, students must possess the skills that allow them to read efficiently and know that they either possess these skills or will soon have them. Competence in reading mathematical text includes understanding the vocabulary and the background or fundamentals of the concepts in the reading. To foster confidence, Vacca and Vacca (1999) suggest that we arouse curiosity, elicit predictions, and urge our students to ask questions about the new content. The prereading strategies and activities presented in this chapter are designed to promote and encourage student readiness and willingness to read mathematical text and content.

As teachers of mathematics, we are often limited by time constraints and the amount of content we are obliged to cover. Some of us may feel that teaching reading is not a priority. However, if we overlook this part of our instruction, we limit the amount of mathematics and diversity of mathematical processes that students might learn. Moreover, if we address the reading of mathematical content initially, we stand a chance of turning out students who are effective readers and, ultimately, successful communicators of mathematics.

Chapter One begins with the review/preview process, which later strategies and activities refer back to. The following prereading strategies and activities are explored in this chapter:

Review/preview process
Knowledge ratings
Anticipation guides
PreP (prereading plan)
Problem-solving prep
Wordsmithing

Review/Preview Process

WHAT? Description

The review/preview process takes place prior to the students' reading of the text. There are two parts to the process: (1) teachers present a review of the prerequisite or background material needed to understand the new content and (2) students preview the new content.

To review the background content, teachers should do one or more of the following:

- Summarize background material.
- Pose a problem from the background material.
- Share a historical anecdote regarding the new concepts.
- Present an interesting problem to be solved after students read and learn the new content.

To preview the assigned reading, students should complete the following tasks:

- Note the title.
- Note all subtitles.
- Note all boxed or highlighted definitions and theorems.
- Note all pictures and graphics.
- Note all other boxed or highlighted special sections, such as biographies of mathematicians or special applications.

WHY? Objectives

The review process allows the mathematics student to:

- Recall necessary mathematical concepts and processes.
- Connect previously learned concepts with new concepts.
- Approach the new content with curiosity and interest.

Previewing allows the mathematics student to:

- Obtain an overview of the reading.
- Pose questions regarding new concepts and anticipate the answers to these questions.
- Delineate or categorize different methods or concepts regarding the main topics from the text.

HOW? Worksheet

The lesson that follows gives a review/preview worksheet that students may use to assist in the review/preview process.

Review/Preview Process

NAME _____ DATE _____

$\pm \cdots \infty \approx \in \infty \varnothing \pm \cdots \infty \approx \in \infty \varnothing \pm \cdots \varnothing \approx \in \infty \varnothing \pm \cdots \in \approx \in \infty \varnothing \pm \cdots \pm \approx \in \infty \varnothing \pm \cdots \infty \approx \in \infty \varnothing$

ASSIGNMENT: Briefly answer the following questions as you preview the section on

_____ on pages _____.

List all titles and subtitles from the new content.
What background concepts do I need to know?
What new concepts and processes do I anticipate learning?
What questions do I have regarding the new content?

Knowledge Ratings

± ··· ∞ ≈ ∈ ∞ ∅ ± ··· ∞ ≈ ∈ ∞ ∅ ± ··· ∅ ≈ ∈ ∞ ∅ ± ··· ∈ ≈ ∈ ∞ ∅ ± ··· ± ≈ ∈ ∞ ∅ ± ··· ∞ ≈ ∈ ∞ ∅

WHAT? Description

Charts that ask the student to assess their prior knowledge are called knowledge ratings (Blachowicz, 1986). The teacher presents students with a list of concepts or topics and surveys their knowledge on these topics. The survey headings for Knowledge Rating charts may take various forms, as the examples that follow show.

WHY? Objectives

Completing the knowledge ratings chart will allow the mathematics student to:

- Self-assess prior knowledge of topics to be studied.
- Target problem areas and make study plans.
- Point out to the teacher personal problem areas.

Reviewing the completed knowledge ratings charts will allow the teacher to:

- Observe problem areas and gaps in learning for students.
- Plan content focus and time allotment for particular topics.
- Find and assign other readings or assignments on problem subjects.

HOW? Example

The following example is from a unit on functions in advanced algebra.

Knowledge Rating for a Unit on Functions

How much do you know about the terms listed in the table? Place an X in the spaces that signal your knowledge.

	A lot!	Some	Not much
Function			
Domain			
Range			
x intercept			
y intercept			
Vertical line test			
Horizontal line test			

Knowledge Ratings: Rating for a College Algebra Course

NAME _____   DATE _____

How much do you know about the equations listed below? Place an X in the spaces that signal your knowledge.

	Can define	**Can give an example**	**Can sketch basic graph**	**Am totally lost**
Linear equation				
Identity equation				
Constant equation				
Quadratic equation				
Polynomial equation				
Rational equation				
Logarithmic equation				
Exponential equation				

My learning goals for this part of the semester are the following:

1. I will _____
2. In terms of studying, I will spend _____ each _____ on studying and homework.
3. I will earn at a(n) _____ on this unit.

_____   _____
signature   date

Knowledge Rating for a Unit on Graphing Rational Functions

NAME _____ DATE _____

Place an X in the spaces for which you agree.

	I can define	I can give an example of	I can graph or find on the graph	I can graph or find on the graph using my graphing calculator
Rational function				
x intercept				
y intercept				
Vertical asymptote				
Horizontal asymptote				
Extrema				

Knowledge Ratings: Template

NAME _____ DATE _____

Topics	A lot!	Some	Not much

Anticipation Guides

WHAT? Description

Anticipation guides (Herber, 1978) are lists of statements that challenge students to explore their knowledge of concepts prior to reading the text and to discover through reading the text's explanation of these concepts.

A mathematical anticipation guide usually contains four to five statements, each with two parts. First, the student is asked to agree or disagree with each statement. Then the student reads the text and determines whether the text or author agrees with each statement.

WHY? Objectives

Anticipation guides allow and motivate mathematics students to:

- Explore their opinions and prior knowledge of mathematical concepts.
- Read closely to find evidence to support their claims or discover the text's view.
- Uncover and identify any misconceptions regarding these concepts.

HOW? Example

Here is an example of an anticipation guide for a section on linear equations in two variables.

Anticipation Guides: Selection on Linear Equations in Two Variables

±···∞≈∈∞∅±···∞≈∈∞∅±···∅≈∈∞∅±···∈≈∈∞∅±···±≈∈∞∅±···∞≈∈∞∅

Directions: In the column labeled ME, place a check next to any statement with which you agree. After reading the section, consider the column labeled TEXT, and place a check next to any statement with which the text agrees.

Me	Text	
_____	_____	1. The solution set for any linear equation in x and y is exactly one ordered pair.
_____	_____	2. The graph of a linear equation is a line.
_____	_____	3. The slope of a vertical line is zero.
_____	_____	4. Slope-intercept form looks like: $y = mx + b$.
_____	_____	5. Two parallel lines have equal slopes.

Anticipation Guides: Solving Quadratic Equations in One Variable

± ·· ∞ ≈ ∈ ∞ ∅ ± ·· ∞ ≈ ∈ ∞ ∅ ± ·· ∅ ≈ ∈ ∞ ∅ ± ·· ∈ ≈ ∈ ∞ ∅ ± ·· ± ≈ ∈ ∞ ∅ ± ·· ∞ ≈ ∈ ∞ ∅

Select the chapter or section in any Algebra II text that discusses solving quadratic equations in one variable. Follow the directions in the anticipation guide below.

Directions: In the column labeled ME, place a check next to any statement with which you agree. After reading the section, consider the column labeled TEXT, and place a check next to any statement with which the text agrees.

Me	**Text**	
_____	_____	1. Quadratic equations have at most two solutions.
_____	_____	2. The quadratic formula can be used to solve any quadratic equation.
_____	_____	3. If $x^2 = 25$, then the solution set for x is {5}.
_____	_____	4. Completing the square is a valid method for solving quadratic equations.
_____	_____	5. When using the factoring method to solve a quadratic equation, you must set the equation equal to zero before you factor.

Anticipation Guides: Measures of Central Tendency

NAME _____ DATE _____

$\pm \cdots \infty \approx \in \infty \varnothing \pm \cdots \infty \approx \in \infty \varnothing \pm \cdots \varnothing \approx \in \infty \varnothing \pm \cdots \in \approx \in \infty \varnothing \pm \cdots \pm \approx \in \infty \varnothing \pm \cdots \infty \approx \in \infty \varnothing$

Directions: In the column labeled ME, place a check next to any statement with which you agree. After reading the section, consider the column labeled TEXT, and place a check next to any statement with which the text agrees.

Me	Text	
_____	_____	1. The median is the middle-most value of a data set.
_____	_____	2. The mean = median = mode of every data set.
_____	_____	3. The mode is the most recurring number in a data set.
_____	_____	4. If the median is more than the mean, then the data set is skewed to the left.
_____	_____	5. If a set contains an even number of data, then the median will be equal to the mean of the two numbers in the middle of the data set.

PreP

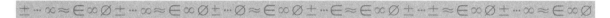

WHAT? Description

The Prereading Plan (PreP) (Langer, 1981) is a large-group brainstorming activity. The teacher guides students in activating, sharing, and fine-tuning prior knowledge. Initially, the teacher chooses one of the key concepts of the reading or lesson and then guides the students in the brainstorming of this concept. Langer suggests that the teacher follow a three-step process to guide the students' collective thoughts:

1. *Initial associations.* The teacher asks, "What comes to mind when you hear _____?" The teacher writes student responses on board.
2. *Secondary reflections.* The teacher asks individual students regarding their responses, "What made you think of _____?" The teacher writes the student reflections under appropriate initial responses on board.
3. *Refining knowledge.* The teacher asks, "Do you have any new ideas or thoughts after hearing your peers' ideas?" The teacher writes new ideas on board.

WHY? Objectives

The PreP allows mathematics students to:

- Activate prior knowledge.
- Hear and reflect on peers' ideas.
- Clarify, refine, and enlarge knowledge.

HOW? Example

The teacher presents the new concept of rational numbers and uses the three-step process in this way:

1. Initial associations

   Fraction

   Whole number

   Not a square root

   Not pi

2. Secondary reflections

   Fraction—fraction of integers

   Whole number—integers

   Not a square root. Could be square root of perfect square.

   Not pi. Pi is a decimal, approximately 3.14, where the decimal digits go on forever and ever with no pattern.

3. Refining knowledge

   A rational number is a fraction of integer over integer.

   Rational numbers are decimals that terminate or have a repeating pattern.

Problem-Solving Prep

± ··· ∞ ≈ ∈ ∞ ∅ ± ··· ∞ ≈ ∈ ∞ ∅ ± ··· ∅ ≈ ∈ ∞ ∅ ± ··· ∈ ≈ ∈ ∞ ∅ ± ··· ± ≈ ∈ ∞ ∅ ± ··· ∞ ≈ ∈ ∞ ∅

The National Council of Supervisors of Mathematics (1988) says that the principal reason for studying mathematics is to learn to solve problems.

WHAT? Description

Problem solving is the process of resolving the confusion or mystery of an unfamiliar situation. The twentieth-century mathematician George Polya devoted his life to helping students become good problem solvers. In his famous book *How to Solve It* (1973), he outlines a four-step process for solving problems:

1. *Understand the problem,* which means read, reread, make a guess, restate the problem, and/or rewrite the question.
2. *Devise a plan,* which means draw a picture, construct a table or graph, use a model, find a pattern, work backward, and/or use a formula or equation appropriate to solving the problem.
3. *Carry out the plan,* which means write out work, solve an equation, and/or recheck work.
4. *Look back,* which means verify or check the solution referring to the initial problem, reread the problem, generalize to larger problem, pose questions for further exploration, and/or compose related problems.

During the problem-solving prep process, students follow a guided reading format to help hone their problem-solving skills. This process may be used prior to or during a section covering applications in an algebra text.

WHY? Objectives

Using the problem-solving prep process, students will:

• Spend time reading problems for understanding.
• Find personal meaning by rewriting problems in their own words.

- Practice using different strategies to solve problems.
- Focus on the understanding phase of problem solving.
- Build confidence in their ability to solve problems.

HOW? Lessons

See the lessons that follow.

Problem-Solving Prep

NAME _____   DATE _____

$\pm \cdots \infty \approx \in \infty \varnothing \pm \cdots \infty \approx \in \infty \varnothing \pm \cdots \varnothing \approx \in \infty \varnothing \pm \cdots \in \approx \in \infty \varnothing \pm \cdots \pm \approx \in \infty \varnothing \pm \cdots \infty \approx \in \infty \varnothing$

ASSIGNMENT: Answer each of the questions below for the written problem. Refer to the following list of problem-solving strategies when answering the "Devise a Plan" question:

- Draw a picture.
- Guess and check.
- Sketch a table or graph.
- Find a pattern.
- Work backward.
- Use a formula or equation.
- Use a model.

Problem: Ten years ago, Sarah paid $80 for a guitar that once belonged to Bob Dylan. Two years ago, she sold it for $90. Last year, she bought it back for $100 and sold it immediately for $110. How much profit did she make?

UNDERSTAND: Rewrite the problem in your own words.
UNDERSTAND: Make a guess, and explain your reasoning.
DEVISE A PLAN: Choose one of the problem-solving strategies listed above.
CARRY OUT PLAN: Use the strategy to solve the problem.
LOOK BACK: Create a similar problem.

Problem-Solving Prep

NAME _____   DATE _____

$\pm \cdots \infty \approx \in \infty \varnothing \pm \cdots \infty \approx \in \infty \varnothing \pm \cdots \varnothing \approx \in \infty \varnothing \pm \cdots \in \approx \in \infty \varnothing \pm \cdots \pm \approx \in \infty \varnothing \pm \cdots \infty \approx \in \infty \varnothing$

ASSIGNMENT: Answer each of the questions below for the written problem. Refer to the following list of problem-solving strategies when answering the "Devise a Plan" question:

- Draw a picture.
- Guess and check.
- Sketch a table or graph.
- Find a pattern.
- Work backward.
- Use a formula or equation.
- Use a model.

Problem: Imagine that the earth is a perfect sphere and its circumference is exactly 25,000 miles at the equator. Now imagine that a band is placed around the earth directly above the equator. The circumference of the band is 10 feet longer than the circumference of the earth. Is it possible to place a 12-inch ruler between the earth and the band?

UNDERSTAND: Rewrite the problem in your own words.
UNDERSTAND: Make a guess, and explain your reasoning.
DEVISE A PLAN: Choose one of the problem-solving strategies listed above.
CARRY OUT PLAN: Use the strategy to solve the problem.
LOOK BACK: Create a similar problem.

Problem-Solving Prep

NAME _____   DATE _____

$\pm\cdots\infty\approx\in\infty\varnothing\pm\cdots\infty\approx\in\infty\varnothing\pm\cdots\varnothing\approx\in\infty\varnothing\pm\cdots\in\approx\in\infty\varnothing\pm\cdots\pm\approx\in\infty\varnothing\pm\cdots\infty\approx\in\infty\varnothing$

ASSIGNMENT: Answer each of the questions below for the written problem. Refer to the following list of problem-solving strategies when answering the "Devise a Plan" question:

- Draw a picture.
- Guess and check.
- Sketch a table or graph.
- Find a pattern.
- Work backward.
- Use a formula or equation.
- Use a model.

Problem: The three Hobbits, Bilbo, Frodo, and Sam, each had a different amount of gold coins. Frodo had twice the amount that Bilbo had. Sam had twice the amount that Frodo had. How many gold coins did each of them have?

UNDERSTAND: Rewrite the problem in your own words.
UNDERSTAND: Make a guess.
DEVISE A PLAN: Choose one of the problem-solving strategies listed above.
CARRY OUT PLAN: Use the strategy to solve the problem.
LOOK BACK: Create a similar problem.

Problem-Solving Prep

Copyright © 2003 by John Wiley & Sons, Inc.

NAME _____   DATE _____

± ⋯ ∞ ≈ ∈ ∞ ∅ ± ⋯ ∞ ≈ ∈ ∞ ∅ ± ⋯ ∅ ≈ ∈ ∞ ∅ ± ⋯ ∈ ≈ ∈ ∞ ∅ ± ⋯ ± ≈ ∈ ∞ ∅ ± ⋯ ∞ ≈ ∈ ∞ ∅

ASSIGNMENT: Answer each of the questions below for the written problem. Refer to the following list of problem-solving strategies when answering the "Devise a Plan" question:

- Draw a picture.
- Guess and check.
- Sketch a table or graph.
- Find a pattern.
- Work backward.
- Use a formula or equation.
- Use a model.

Problem: A man put one pair of rabbits in a certain place entirely surrounded by a wall. How many pairs of rabbits can be produced from that pair in a year if the nature of these rabbits is such that every month, each pair bears a new pair, which from the second month on becomes productive?

UNDERSTAND: Rewrite the problem in your own words.
UNDERSTAND: Make a guess.
DEVISE A PLAN: Choose one of the problem-solving strategies listed above.
CARRY OUT PLAN: Use the strategy to solve the problem.
LOOK BACK: Create a similar problem.

Algebra Out Loud

Wordsmithing

$\pm \cdots \infty \approx \in \infty \varnothing \pm \cdots \infty \approx \in \infty \varnothing \pm \cdots \varnothing \approx \in \infty \varnothing \pm \cdots \in \approx \in \infty \varnothing \pm \cdots \pm \approx \in \infty \varnothing \pm \cdots \infty \approx \in \infty \varnothing$

WHAT? Description

A *wordsmith* is a person who coins new words. Writers are often collectors of words. An author who considers herself a wordsmith experiments with new words or uses words in ways that are somewhat unusual. For example, a graphing calculator might be referred to as a *graphulator*. The wordsmithing activity has the student actively searching for new words and considering what these words mean. Because much of the mathematics in algebra texts builds off the prior lesson (that is, it is recursive), students often discover this is true of the vocabulary of algebra.

In this activity, the student scans the new content in the text, searching for new algebraic words. As she discovers a new word, she writes it on a sheet of paper containing a three-column matrix, leaving two of the columns blank. After completing her list of new terms, the student guesses what each word means and writes this definition or description in the cell next to the word. Then, after reading the assigned content or lesson, she fills out the cells in the final column of the matrix with the correct definitions. If the wordsmithing activity is repeated often enough, students can become quite adept at guessing the meanings of the new words.

WHY? Objectives

After completing the wordsmithing activity, students will:

- Learn the definitions of new words.
- Become good at defining terms in their own words.
- Become better readers, for they must read carefully to find the definitions of the new words.
- Become algebraic wordsmiths.

HOW? Examples

See the lessons for matrices.

Wordsmithing: Matrix

NAME _____   DATE _____

± ⋯ ∞ ≈ ∈ ∞ ∅ ± ⋯ ∞ ≈ ∈ ∞ ∅ ± ⋯ ∅ ≈ ∈ ∞ ∅ ± ⋯ ∈ ≈ ∈ ∞ ∅ ± ⋯ ± ≈ ∈ ∞ ∅ ± ⋯ ∞ ≈ ∈ ∞ ∅

Chapter _____ on pages _____.

New term	Your initial definition	The text's definition

Algebra Out Loud

Wordsmithing: Matrix

NAME _____   DATE _____

± ∙∙ ∞ ≈ ∈ ∞ ∅ ± ∙∙ ∞ ≈ ∈ ∞ ∅ ± ∙∙ ∅ ≈ ∈ ∞ ∅ ± ∙∙ ∈ ≈ ∈ ∞ ∅ ± ∙∙ ± ≈ ∈ ∞ ∅ ± ∙∙ ∞ ≈ ∈ ∞ ∅

ASSIGNMENT: Guess what the terms mean, and write your guess in column 2. Then use the text to find the correct definition, and write it in column 3.

New term	Your initial definition	The text's definition
Function		
Linear function		
Constant function		
Identity function		
Domain		
Range		
One-to-one function		

Reading and Vocabulary-Building Strategies and Activities

Prelude

Mathematical text is unique in that the images and ideas conjured up by reading are quantitative in nature. The reading of mathematical content should be an active and interactive learning process.

Active reading means that the reader visualizes concepts, organizes information, poses questions, predicts solutions or new knowledge, and makes connections with prior knowledge. During this process, the reader makes personal meaning of the content and thus gains ownership of the new knowledge.

The interactive learning component of reading mathematical text consists of the student's writing and talking about mathematics. Writing about mathematics helps the reader to set goals, consider the audience, organize and refine thinking, and summarize and share new knowledge. Talking about mathematics allows the student to compare thinking, obtain and share new ideas, guide and be guided in the reflection and study processes, and see the concepts in a new light.

The strategies and activities contained in this chapter focus on the reading process and on vocabulary building while reading the text. The goals for these activities consist of helping students to:

- Connect prior and new knowledge.
- Reinforce and enlarge vocabulary.

- Break up information into smaller, more manageable pieces.
- Categorize and organize information.
- Select key concepts.
- Interpret definitions, theorems, and processes.
- Follow and generalize from examples.
- Construct study guides.

This chapter explores the following activities:

- Magic square activity
- Concept circles
- K-W-L
- Semantic feature analysis
- Graphic organizers
- Reading math symbols
- Proof reading
- Semantic word maps

Magic Square Activity

WHAT? Description

The magic square activity combines a matching activity with the intrigue and mathematics of a magic square (Vacca and Vacca, 1999). The write-up of the matching activity consists of two columns: one for concepts and one for definitions, facts, examples, or descriptions. As the student solves the matching activity, he or she places the correct number next to the letter in each square inside the magic square using the following form:

A	**B**	**C**
D	**E**	**F**
G	**H**	**I**

To see if the answers are correct, the student adds the numbers in each row, in each column, and in each diagonal. These sums should be equal (although in some cases, the diagonal does not yield the magic number). This sum is referred to as the square's *magic number*.

WHY? Objectives

The magic square activity is used to:

- Reinforce concept or word meaning.
- Interject interest and mystery into what might be considered a mundane activity.
- Introduce the concept and properties of magic squares.

The magic square examples that follow use the magic number of 15:

7	3	5
2	4	9
6	8	1

8	1	6
3	5	7
4	9	2

6	1	8
7	5	3
2	9	4

The magic square example that follows uses the magic number of 39. Note that in this case, the diagonal sums do not yield same sum as rows and columns.

2	7	18	12
8	5	11	15
13	17	6	3
16	10	4	9

Magic Square Activity: Divisibility Rules

NAME _____ DATE _____

ASSIGNMENT: Select the best answer for each of the terms on the left from the numbered rules on the right. Put the number in the proper square in the magic square. Add each row, and add each column. If these sums are the same number, then you have found the magic number and matched the correct terms with their rules.

Concepts	Rules
A. Divisibility by 2	1. Sum of even-numbered digits minus sum of odd-numbered digits is divisible by 11.
B. Divisibility by 3	2. Unit's digit is 0 or 5.
C. Divisibility by 4	3. Sum of digits is divisible by 3.
D. Divisibility by 5	4. Number is divisible by 2 and 3.
E. Divisibility by 6	5. The number formed by the last two digits is divisible by 4.
F. Divisibility by 8	6. Sum of all digits is divisible by 9.
G. Divisibility by 9	7. Unit's digit is 0, 2, 4, 6, or 8.
H. Divisibility by 10	8. Unit's digit is 0.
I. Divisibility by 11	9. The number formed by the last 3 digits is divisible by 8.

Magic Square

A	B	C
D	E	F
G	H	I

Magic number = _____

Concept Circles

WHAT? Description

Concept circles are one of the more versatile reading and postreading activities (Vacca and Vacca, 1999). A concept circle usually focuses on one concept and its important features. Features or descriptors of the concept are placed in sectors of the circle, which is generally divided into quarters (although more sectors may be used).

Concept circles may be teacher created and used to quiz students—for example:

- Given the descriptors contained in the sections of the circle, students identify the concept.
- Given the concept and descriptors, students select which of the descriptors is incorrect.
- Given the concept and a few descriptors, students fill in the rest of the circle.

Concept circles also may be student created—for example:

- The teacher gives the concept, and students fill in the sections of the circle.
- The student selects the concept from the reading and fills in the sections of the circle.

WHY? Objectives

The use of concept circles allows the mathematics student to:

- Categorize information from the reading.
- Review features and descriptors of a certain concept.
- Self-assess reading comprehension.

This example uses a geometric concept circle:

4 congruent sides	exactly 2 distinct pairs of opposite and congruent angles
non-regular quadrilateral	diagonals bisect each other

The concept described is a

_____

Concept Circles

± ⋯ ∞ ≈ ∈ ∞ ∅ ± ⋯ ∞ ≈ ∈ ∞ ∅ ± ⋯ ∅ ≈ ∈ ∞ ∅ ± ⋯ ∈ ≈ ∈ ∞ ∅ ± ⋯ ± ≈ ∈ ∞ ∅ ± ⋯ ∞ ≈ ∈ ∞ ∅

The concept is _____ .

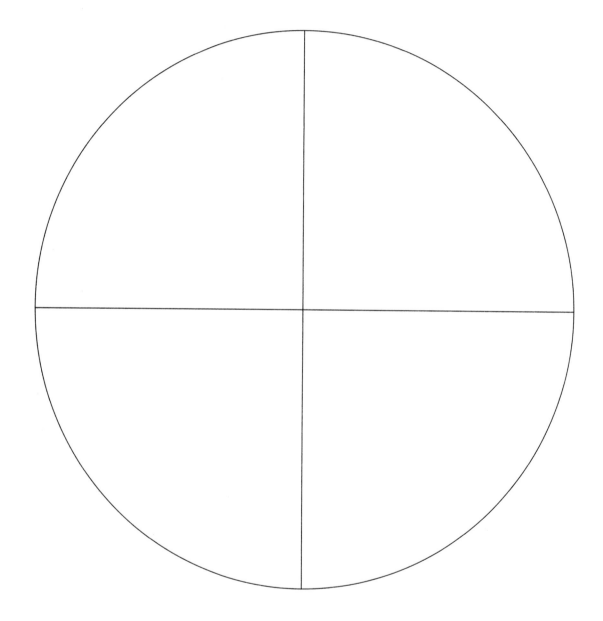

K-W-L

WHAT? Description

K-W-L (Ogle, 1986) is a reading strategy involving note taking prior to, during, and after reading:

> *K* stands for "What I *K*now"
>
> *W* stands for "What I *W*ant to Know"
>
> *L* stands for "What I *L*earned"

Students write notes in a three-column grid, using the following format:

K What I **know**	W What I **want** to know	L What I **learned**
During prereading, write notes about what you already know regarding the concepts presented.	*During prereading, write questions about what you want to know regarding the concepts presented.*	*As you read or after reading, write answers to questions posed in the "What I want to know" column, or notes regarding what you have learned.*

WHY? Objectives

K-W-L allows the student to:

- Reflect on prior and new knowledge.
- Merge prior knowledge with new knowledge.
- Summarize prior and new knowledge.
- Authentically assess (self-assess) his or her own learning process.

Use the K-W-L reading strategy prior to, during, and after you read the following narrative regarding the Golden Ratio:

Fibonacci, the Greeks, and a Divine Ratio

Leonardo Fibonacci was an Italian mathematician who lived during the Middle Ages. While contemplating the mating habits of a pair of rabbits and their descendants, Fibonacci created the following sequence:

$$1, 1, 2, 3, 5, 8, 13, 21, 34, 55, 89, 144, \ldots$$

The Fibonacci sequence is a recursive sequence. Starting with the third term, each term is the sum of the two terms preceding it:

$$1 + 1 = 2, \quad 1 + 2 = 3, \quad 2 + 3 = 5, \quad 3 + 5 = 8, \quad 5 + 8 = 13, \quad 8 + 13 = 21, \ldots$$

This sequence has many extraordinary properties. One pertains to the ratios of consecutive pairs. Note the following ratios:

$1/1 = 1$

$\frac{1}{2} = .5$

$2/3 = .666 \ldots$

$3/5 = .6$

$5/8 = .625$

$8/13 = .6153846154$

$13/21 \sim .619047619$

$21/34 \sim .6176470588$

If we were to continue in this pattern, we would see that the ratios would tend toward (get closer and closer to) the irrational number $\frac{\sqrt{5}-1}{2} \approx .6180339887\ldots$ Note that the consecutive ratios vacillate between being either smaller than or larger than .6180339887.

Fibonacci was delighted to discover his sequence contained this special property. He knew that the Greeks had long thought of this ratio as a divine number and had aptly titled it the Golden Ratio. As early as 350 B.C., Greek artists and architects believed that figures and structures displaying proportions that approximated this ratio were very pleasing to the eye. The Parthenon in Athens, Greece, was built with many features using dimensions whose ratios tend toward the Golden Ratio. For example, the height compared to the width of the front of the Parthenon approximated .618. Also, many sculptures of Greek gods and goddesses displayed proportions close to this divine ratio.

To see if you have goddess- or god-like proportions, use the formula below:

$$r = \frac{(navel)\,height}{height}$$

(Your navel height is the distance from the floor to your belly button.) If your ratio is close to the Golden Ratio of .618, then you are proportionally divine, at least by Fibonacci and the ancient Greeks' standards!

The following table shows how the K-W-L strategy can be applied to the reading. Note that the K and W columns are completed prior to reading and the L column is completed during and after reading the piece.

K What I **know**	W What I **want** to know	L What I **learned**
A ratio is a fraction.	*Why is the Golden Ratio considered divine?*	*The Greeks used this ratio in their famous sculptures and buildings.*
Fibonacci invented a sequence.	*How is the Fibonacci sequence related to the Golden Ratio?*	*Consecutive pairs form ratios that tend to the Golden Ratio.*

K-W-L

Copyright © 2003 by John Wiley & Sons, Inc.

NAME _____   DATE _____

The K-W-L Reading Strategy follows the format below:

K What I **k**now	W What I **w**ant to know	L What I **l**earned
During prereading, write questions about what you already know regarding the concepts presented.	*During prereading, write questions about what you want to know regarding the concepts presented.*	*As you read or after reading, write answers to questions posed in the "What I want to know" column, or notes regarding what you have learned.*

ASSIGNMENT: Use the reading titled _____
on page _____ to complete the table below:

K What I **k**now	W What I **w**ant to know	L What I **l**earned

Algebra Out Loud

Semantic Feature Analysis

± ··· ∞ ≈ ∈ ∞ ∅ ± ··· ∞ ≈ ∈ ∞ ∅ ± ··· ∅ ≈ ∈ ∞ ∅ ± ··· ∈ ≈ ∈ ∞ ∅ ± ··· ± ≈ ∈ ∞ ∅ ± ··· ∞ ≈ ∈ ∞ ∅

WHAT? Description

Semantic feature analysis (Baldwin, Ford, and Readance, 1981) is a reading strategy that has students complete a matrix showing how various terms and concepts are alike or different. The terms or concepts are related or fall under a particular category. The matrix itself consists of several columns. The first column contains a listing of the terms. The remaining columns contain headings spelling out features that the terms or concepts might have in common.

WHY? Objectives

Semantic feature analysis allows the mathematics student to:

- Explore features of certain mathematical concepts.
- Compare and contrast features of related mathematical concepts.
- Summarize this information.
- Refer back to the completed matrix when reviewing for exams.

HOW? Example

Note that an X placed in a particular space indicates that the given feature applies to the given quadrilateral. If the best response is "not necessarily," the space is left blank.

Quadrilateral	4-sided polygon	Opposite sides are congruent	Opposite sides are parallel	Exactly one pair of parallel sides	Vertex angles are congruent
Square	X	X	X		X
Rectangle	X	X	X		X
Parallelogram	X	X	X		
Rhombus	X	X	X		
Trapezoid	X			X	

Another version of semantic feature analysis has the student fill in answers to questions regarding various features of related concepts. See the lessons that follow.

Semantic Feature Analysis

NAME _____   DATE _____

± ·· ∞ ≈ ∈ ∞ ∅ ± ·· ∞ ≈ ∈ ∞ ∅ ± ·· ∅ ≈ ∈ ∞ ∅ ± ·· ∈ ≈ ∈ ∞ ∅ ± ·· ± ≈ ∈ ∞ ∅ ± ·· ∞ ≈ ∈ ∞ ∅

Fill in each of the cells with the correct answers.

Functions	Number of zeros possible	Describe general shape of graph	Sketch general shape of graph	Number of extrema possible
Linear function				
Constant function				
Quadratic function				
Cubic function				
Polynomial function				

Semantic Feature Analysis

NAME _____ DATE _____

± ·· ∞ ≈ ∈ ∞ ∅ ± ·· ∞ ≈ ∈ ∞ ∅ ± ·· ∅ ≈ ∈ ∞ ∅ ± ·· ∈ ≈ ∈ ∞ ∅ ± ·· ± ≈ ∈ ∞ ∅ ± ·· ∞ ≈ ∈ ∞ ∅

Place an X in the space provided if the indicated feature applies to the given concept.

Graph of given equation	Has a max	Has a min	Is increasing, then decreasing left to right	Is decreasing, then increasing left to right	Is concave up	Is concave down
$y = x^2 - 9$						
$y = x^2 + 9$						
$y = x^2 + 2x + 1$						
$y = x^2 - 2x - 24$						
$y = x^2 + 7x + 12$						

Fill in each cell with the correct answer, if one exists. If there is not a correct answer, write NA.

Graph of given equation	Give the max, if it exists	Give the min, if it exists	List all zeros	Give the y intercept	Give all intervals where y is increasing	Give all intervals where y is decreasing
$y = x^2 - 9$						
$y = x^2 + 9$						
$y = x^2 + 2x + 1$						
$y = x^2 - 2x - 24$						
$y = x^2 + 7x + 12$						

Semantic Feature Analysis

NAME _____   DATE _____

Fill in the matrix by answering each question as it pertains to the given algebraic concept.

Equations	Degree?	Number of distinct zeros?	Shape of graph?	Number of y intercepts?	Number of x intercepts?
Linear					
Quadratic					
Cubic					
Polynomial	nth				

Algebra Out Loud

Semantic Feature Analysis

NAME _____   DATE _____

Place an X in the space provided if the indicated feature applies to the given concept. If the best response is "not necessarily," leave the space blank.

	Domain = all reals	**Domain = $x \geq 0$**	**Domain = $x > 0$**	**Has an asymptote**
Exponential function				
Logarithmic function				
Rational function				
Polynomial function				

Fill in the cells with the correct information regarding the features of each of the four functions.

	Write out the general form in letters	**Write an example with actual numbers**	**Describe the basic shape of the graph**	**Describe any asymptotes in the graph of the general form**
Exponential function				
Logarithmic function				
Rational function				
Polynomial function				

Semantic Feature Analysis

NAME _____ DATE _____

Place an X in the space provided if the indicated feature applies to the given statistical concept. If the best response is "not necessarily," leave the space blank.

Descriptive statistics	Measures of central tendency	Measures of dispersion	Statistic as an exact value(s) from the data set
Mean			
Median			
Mode			
Standard deviation			
Variance			
Range			

Algebra Out Loud

Semantic Feature Analysis

NAME _____   DATE _____

Fill in the matrix by answering each question yes or no as it pertains to the given large set of numbers.

Sets	Is an infinite set	Is a subset of the set above it	Has an additive identity in its set	Has a multiplicative identity in its set
Complex numbers				
Real numbers				
Rational numbers				
Integers				
Whole numbers				
Natural numbers				
Irrational numbers				

Semantic Feature Analysis

NAME _____   DATE _____

$\pm \cdots \infty \approx \in \infty \varnothing \pm \cdots \infty \approx \in \infty \varnothing \pm \cdots \varnothing \approx \in \infty \varnothing \pm \cdots \in \approx \in \infty \varnothing \pm \cdots \pm \approx \in \infty \varnothing \pm \cdots \infty \approx \in \infty \varnothing$

Answer yes or no to the question implied in each cell. In the last column, write out another name for each process.

	May use prime factorization to find	May be used to add or subtract fractions	May be used to factor	Write another name for
Least common multiple (LCM)				
Greatest common factor (GCF)				

Use either the LCM or the GCF to solve the following problems:

1. $\dfrac{3}{16} + \dfrac{5}{24}$

2. Factor: $36xy - 12x^2y + 52x^3y^2$

Graphic Organizers

± ·· ∞ ≈ ∈ ∞ ∅ ± ·· ∞ ≈ ∈ ∞ ∅ ± · ∅ ≈ ∈ ∞ ∅ ± ·· ∈ ≈ ∈ ∞ ∅ ± ·· ± ≈ ∈ ∞ ∅ ± ·· ∞ ≈ ∈ ∞ ∅

WHAT? Description

Graphic organizers (Barron, 1969) are schematics created to show connections between key concepts. Mathematical graphic organizers often are constructed using some mathematical figure or graphic.

Graphic organizers may be created by the teacher or a student. They may be used during prereading, reading, or postreading. Teachers might present a graphic organizer to the class as a prereading demonstration to elicit students' prior knowledge of the concepts to be studied. Working in groups, students might brainstorm terms related to some larger concept and create their own graphic organizers.

WHY? Objectives

Graphic organizers are used to assist the mathematics student to:

- Activate prior knowledge of concepts.
- Make effective connections between key concepts.
- Summarize or organize main ideas from the reading for reviewing purposes.

HOW? Example

This example is of a teacher-created graphic organizer using the following terms:

3rd quartile

maximum

box plot

median

minimum

1st quartile

Box Plot Graphic

minimum

1st quartile

— median —

3rd quartile

maximum

Graphic Organizers

$\pm \cdots \infty \approx \in \infty \varnothing \pm \cdots \infty \approx \in \infty \varnothing \pm \cdots \varnothing \approx \in \infty \varnothing \pm \cdots \in \approx \in \infty \varnothing \pm \cdots \pm \approx \in \infty \varnothing \pm \cdots \infty \approx \in \infty \varnothing$

ASSIGNMENT

1. Scan the list of terms below.
2. Write each term on a 3- by 5-inch index card.
3. Select the term(s) that all of the other terms might fall under.
4. Sort the cards/terms, and place the cards showing the connections between the terms.
5. Choose an appropriate mathematical figure (for example, a square or circle), and sketch the organizer, writing the terms in the proper sites.

Remember there is not just one way to complete this assignment. Be creative!

Terms

circumference
circle
diameter
secant line
radius
diameter
area
tangent line
chord
sector
arc

Graphic Organizers

NAME _____ DATE _____

ASSIGNMENT: Fill in the blanks with features and/or descriptors of pi that fit the category at the top of each caption.

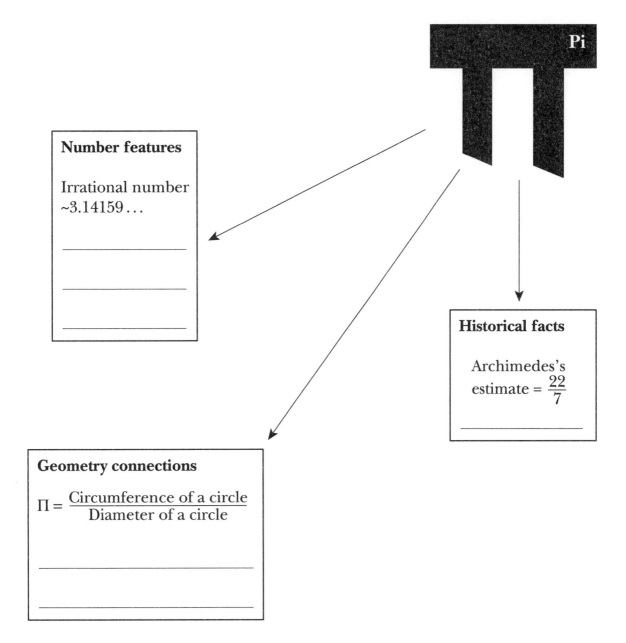

Number features

Irrational number
~3.14159 . . .

_____

_____

_____

Historical facts

Archimedes's
estimate = $\frac{22}{7}$

_____

Geometry connections

$\Pi = \dfrac{\text{Circumference of a circle}}{\text{Diameter of a circle}}$

_____

_____

Reading Math Symbols

WHAT? Description

Creating a witty short story using math symbols is one way of reinforcing student recognition of these symbols. For example, consider the following symbols:

∞	infinity	$\exists$	there exists
$\approx$	approximately equal to	$\pm$	plus or minus
$\rightarrow$	implies	$\forall$	for all
$\leftrightarrow$	if and only if	$\therefore$	therefore
$\in$	is an element of	...	goes on forever
$\neq$	is not equal to	$\varnothing$	empty set

WHY? Objectives

Requiring students to use math symbols to create a story will:

- Reinforce the meaning of the symbols.
- Promote reflection and retention of math symbols.

HOW? Example

Here is an example of a short story using the symbols:

In the Land of ∞, $\exists$ a melancholy creature
who was not $\in$ of any particular set or sect.
$\forall$ the creature's desires to be a part of a sect,
she felt she was $\neq$ the other creatures of ∞.
$\leftrightarrow$ she was prettier and smarter, then
she could be an $\in$ of some set besides $\varnothing$.
$\therefore$ she decided that she would ... in her humble efforts
+ remain a unique creature in the Land of ∞.

Proof Reading

± ··· ∞ ≈ ∈ ∞ ∅ ± ··· ∞ ≈ ∈ ∞ ∅ ± ··· ∅ ≈ ∈ ∞ ∅ ± ··· ∈ ≈ ∈ ∞ ∅ ± ··· ± ≈ ∈ ∞ ∅ ± ··· ∞ ≈ ∈ ∞ ∅

WHAT? Description

Proof reading is an activity designed for introducing students to mathematical proof. Without proof, we are likely to arrive at incorrect conclusions. In 1988, the National Council of Supervisors of Mathematics suggested that teachers move away from two-column proofs to short sequences of theorems written in paragraph or sentence form. Eventually, the student will need to know how to read and to compose this type of proof. To succeed in this, students must understand definitions and logic and have the insight and ability to make connections between theorems and concepts. The proof reading activity is a good starting point for developing these skills.

The proof reading activity encourages students to look at mathematical statements in various forms. Ideally, students refashion these statements in four formats: verbal, numerical, visual, and algebraic. It should be pointed out to the student that the numerical form only gives particular cases, while the visual and algebraic forms give the general cases that constitute proofs.

For example, let ☺ = unknown number and • = a constant:

Verbal form:	Add 3 to a number.
Visual form:	☺•••
Numerical form:	[if the number = 4] $4 + 3 = 7$
Algebraic form:	$x + 3$

WHY? Objectives

The proof reading activity will:

- Introduce the mathematics student to the rudiments of proof.
- Give the mathematics student practice with basic proof writing and reading.
- Allow the mathematics student to see what forms constitute proof.
- Encourage the mathematics student to consider various approaches to proof writing.
- Allow the mathematics student to make connections between mathematical statements.

The examples that follow allow students to examine algebraic proofs in the various formats: numerical, visual, and algebraic.

Example 1

Consider the mathematical "trick" spelled out in the first column of the table below. The answer will be your original number.

Verbal	Numerical (one case)	Visual (geometric proof)	Algebraic (algebraic proof)
Pick a number.	2	☺	x
Add 3 to the number.	$2 + 3 = 5$	☺●●●	$x + 3$
Multiply by 2.	$2 \times 5 = 10$	☺●●●☺●●●	$2(x + 3) = 2x + 6$
Subtract 6.	$10 - 6 = 4$	☺☺	$2x + 6 - 6 = 2x$
Take $\frac{1}{2}$ of the result.	$\frac{1}{2}$ of $4 = 2$	☺	$\frac{1}{2}(2x) = x$

After students complete a few tables similar to the one above, they should be able to create their own math trick.

Example 2

Prove: $(a + b)^2 = a^2 + 2ab + b^2$

Numerical: This gives one case:

$$\text{Let } a = 2 \text{ and } b = 3$$
$$(2 + 3)^2 = 5^2 = 25$$
$$2^2 + 2(2)(3) + 3^2 = 4 + 12 + 9 = 25$$

Visual: This is a geometric proof, originating with the ancient Greeks:

Note: The sides are of length A + B. So the area of the square is
(A + B) (A + B)
$= A^2 + (A \times B) + (A \times B) + B^2$
$= A^2 + 2(A \times B) + B^2$

Example 3

Prove:

$$\cot x = \frac{1 + \cos x}{\sin x + \tan x}$$

Algebraic: Proving trigonometry identities are good beginning proofs for students. The idea is to break everything down into its most basic identity. Then, using a sequence of equivalent trigonometric identities, complete the algebra:

$$\frac{1 + \cos x}{\sin x + \tan x} = \frac{1 + \cos x}{\sin x + (\sin x / \cos x)}$$

Visual: The geometric proof involves the use of a graphing calculator:

Let $y_1 = \cot x$

and

$$y_2 = \frac{1 + \cos x}{\sin x + \tan x}$$

Immediately, students will see that y_1 is the same graph as y_2.

Having students consider how the calculator solves this type of problem makes for quality reflection on and a lively discussion about algorithms and technology.

Proof Reading

NAME _____   DATE _____

± ⋯ ∞ ≈ ∈ ∞ ∅ ± ⋯ ∞ ≈ ∈ ∞ ∅ ± ⋯ ∅ ≈ ∈ ∞ ∅ ± ⋯ ∈ ≈ ∈ ∞ ∅ ± ⋯ ± ≈ ∈ ∞ ∅ ± ⋯ ∞ ≈ ∈ ∞ ∅

Consider the mathematical trick given in the verbal column of the table below. Fill in the last three columns.

Verbal	Numerical	Visual or geometric	Algebraic
Pick a number.			
Add 3.			
Multiply by 2.			
Take $\frac{1}{2}$ of the result.			
Subtract your original number.			

The result will always be _____.

EXTENSION: Devise a mathematical trick of your own, and show why it works.

Semantic Word Maps

$\pm \cdots \infty \approx \in \infty \varnothing \pm \cdots \infty \approx \in \infty \varnothing \pm \cdots \varnothing \approx \in \infty \varnothing \pm \cdots \in \approx \in \infty \varnothing \pm \cdots \pm \approx \in \infty \varnothing \pm \cdots \infty \approx \in \infty \varnothing$

WHAT? Description

Semantic word maps are graphics used to depict and display relationships between key concepts and terms. The semantic word map often resembles a flowchart or a web connecting mathematical terms. Arrows connect related concepts and often display a hierarchy of the terms.

WHY? Objectives

Constructing semantic word maps allows the mathematics student to:

- Explore relationships between mathematical concepts and terms.
- Consider the hierarchy of key concepts.
- Create study guides displaying key concepts.

HOW? Example

Consider the following related algebraic concepts:

linear

quadratic

polynomial

equations

line

cubic

parabola

graphs

equations

First, we note that the two main concepts seem to be "equations" and "graphs," and they are related. The remaining terms appear to be either types of equations or types of graphs. The following semantic word map clearly shows the relationship between and the hierarchy of the terms:

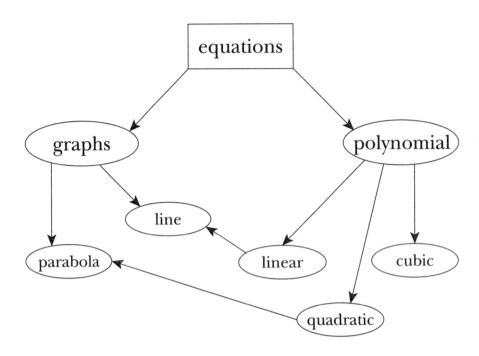

Semantic Word Maps

± ⋯ ∞ ≈ ∈ ∞ ∅ ± ⋯ ∞ ≈ ∈ ∞ ∅ ± ⋯ ∅ ≈ ∈ ∞ ∅ ± ⋯ ∈ ≈ ∈ ∞ ∅ ± ⋯ ± ≈ ∈ ∞ ∅ ± ⋯ ∞ ≈ ∈ ∞ ∅

Sketch a semantic word map showing the relationship and hierarchy of these terms:

exponential function
logarithmic function
domain
range
vertical asymptote
horizontal asymptote
base
power
e
argument
x intercept
y intercept
(0,1)
(1,0)
common logarithm
natural logarithm

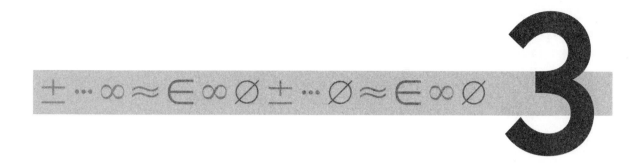

Postreading Strategies and Activities

Prelude

The goal of postreading strategies and activities is to foster student learning and retention of mathematical content. Learning entails setting goals, linking old and new knowledge, organizing information, and reflecting on the learning process. The strategies and activities in this chapter reinforce these cognitive and technical skills and promote effective study habits.

Vacca and Vacca (1998) suggest there are three levels of comprehension or learning: literal (reading the text), interpretive (reading between the lines of the text), and applied (reading beyond the lines of the text). Often mathematics students confuse memorizing with learning. Although some rote learning is necessary in mathematics, it is only one small part of the picture. Reflection and communication are needed for retention. All in all, learning is mental aerobics and must be an active experience. The strategies and activities in this chapter take the student beyond memorizing and enhance active learning.

Chapter Three explores the following activities:

Group speak

Concept cards

Frayer model

Question–answer relationship (QAR)

Comparison and contrast matrix

Group Speak

± ··· ∞ ≈ ∈ ∞ ∅ ± ··· ∞ ≈ ∈ ∞ ∅ ± ··· ∅ ≈ ∈ ∞ ∅ ± ··· ∈ ≈ ∈ ∞ ∅ ± ··· ± ≈ ∈ ∞ ∅ ± ··· ∞ ≈ ∈ ∞ ∅

WHAT? Description

Group speak is a large-group summarizing and paraphrasing strategy. Students are encouraged to think out loud during this activity. The teacher guides the large group of students in reviewing the content previously read. This activity works well at the end of a chapter or just prior to an exam. The teacher starts the discussion with a question like, "Class, what do you consider to be the major concepts from this unit?" After the students respond by giving several of the key concepts, the teacher asks for features or examples of each of the key concepts.

Given the right prompts, this large-group activity can evolve into a group brainstorming activity. Students might be asked to give real-world examples of algebraic or geometric concepts. For example, a group speak discussion focused on the imaginary unit "i." When asked about the usefulness of this concept, a student gave the response, "I have heard that electrical engineers use complex numbers." Several students asked how. This was an opportunity for the teacher to guide the group in considering the quadratic equations that yield complex solutions and their connection to parabolic curves and electrical circuits.

The teacher or students may use graphic organizers to summarize the concepts and related information gleaned from the group speak discussion. Example 2 (in the "HOW" section) shows a graphic organizer containing the information from a large-group discussion on linear equations.

WHY? Objectives

Group speak is a postreading activity that allows the mathematics student to:

- Review key concepts for upcoming assessments.
- Reflect on and paraphrase content.
- Hear peers' rephrasing or rewording of the content.
- "Think out loud" in a guided discussion or review of content.

HOW? Examples

The examples are of a group speak summary of key concepts and a group speak summary of a lesson.

Example 1

This example is a group speak summary of key concepts from "A Mod Squad of 6." (The reading is on page 64.) These are the major topics:

> clock arithmetic
>
> modulus
>
> mod 6
>
> congruence
>
> conversions
>
> base n
>
> mod addition
>
> mod subtraction
>
> additive identity

Example 2

This example uses a graphic organizer showing a group speak summary of a lesson on linear equations:

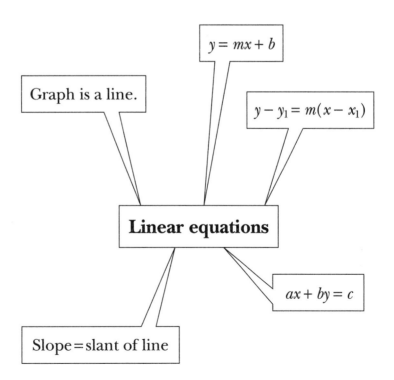

Concept Cards

± ⋯ ∞ ≈ ∈ ∞ ∅ ± ⋯ ∞ ≈ ∈ ∞ ∅ ± ⋯ ∅ ≈ ∈ ∞ ∅ ± ⋯ ∈ ≈ ∈ ∞ ∅ ± ⋯ ± ≈ ∈ ∞ ∅ ± ⋯ ∞ ≈ ∈ ∞ ∅

WHAT? Description

The construction of concept cards is a vocabulary- or concept-building activity. Students use 3- by 5-inch index cards to catalogue key concepts and terms. The concept is written on one side of the card and its definition and a clarifying example on the other side. The concept cards may be used as study material or in the construction of a math glossary.

Merriam-Webster's Collegiate Dictionary defines *glossary* as "a list of difficult, technical, or foreign terms with definitions . . . as for some particular . . . field of knowledge." Glossaries often are found at the end of textbooks, with terms listed in alphabetical order. Students who write out concept definitions in words that make sense to them are more likely to remember and better communicate this knowledge.

WHY? Objectives

The construction and use of concept cards assists the mathematics student in:

- Identifying the key concepts and terms from the text.
- Defining the concepts in his or her words, promoting ownership of knowledge.
- Creating a powerful study guide for preassessment purposes.
- Creating a mathematics glossary for future use.

HOW? Example

This example is contained in a lesson:

A Mod Squad of 6
It is 9 A.M. and in 6 hours, Bernie is to report to work. If Bernie is in the air force, he will report to work at 1500, military time. However, since Bernie uses regular time, he should arrive at work at 3 P.M.

This is an example of clock arithmetic. We begin learning clock arithmetic (or how to tell time) in kindergarten. Let us consider a world where clocks contain only 6 hours. If it is 4:00, then 6 hours later, it would be 4:00 again. Of course, it is easy to see the problems that we would encounter if our clocks contained only 6 hours. However, exploring a number system that contains only 6 digits, as opposed to our 10-digit number system, may prove an interesting experience. (A digit is a one-symbol number.)

The base 10 digits are 0, 1, 2, 3, 4, 5, 6, 7, 8, and 9. Consider a world where the only digits that exist are 0, 1, 2, 3, 4, 5. We express each number in the following form: 2(mod 6) or 5(mod 6). *Mod* stands for modulus. If we were to convert our base 10 numbers to mod 6 numbers, we would do something like this:

$$9 \cong 3(\text{mod } 6)$$
$$7 \cong 1(\text{mod } 6)$$

The symbol $\cong$ stands for "is congruent to," which means "is equivalent to" or "has the same value or worth."

The rule is *$a \cong b$(mod 6) if $a - b$ is a multiple of 6.* (Note that b is limited to the digits 0 to 6.)

An example is $14 \cong \underline{\quad}$ (mod 6). Consider the following multiples of 6: 0, 6, 12, 18, 24, . . . We try $14 - x = 0$, which gives $x = 14$, but 14 is not a valid mod 6 number.

$$14 - x = 6 \text{ gives } x = 8.$$
$$14 - x = 12 \text{ gives } x = 2, \text{ which is a valid mod 6 digit.}$$

Thus, $14 \cong 2$ (mod 6).

We are looking for all the mod 6 digits that when replacing the blank in $14 \cong \underline{\quad}$ (mod 6) it becomes a true statement. Often, the easiest way to do this is to try all digits 0 through 5 in the congruency.

Now, you try the following:

$$12 \cong \underline{\quad} (\text{mod } 6)$$
$$21 \cong \underline{\quad} (\text{mod } 6)$$
$$53 \cong \underline{\quad} (\text{mod } 6)$$

Modulus 6 is a number system of base 6. Our number system is considered base 10. Generally, a base n system contains n digits. A valid base n number is any of the digits from 0 to $n-1$. The following theorem gives a rule for finding congruencies:

Theorem: $a \cong b(\mod n)$ if $a - b$ is a multiple of n.

Try the following:

$$9 \cong \underline{\hspace{1cm}} (\mod 8)$$
$$18 \cong \underline{\hspace{1cm}} (\mod 5)$$
$$23 \cong \underline{\hspace{1cm}} (\mod 12)$$
$$101 \cong \underline{\hspace{1cm}} (\mod 10)$$

Modulus 6 numbers can be added or subtracted. One approach is to add or subtract the two numbers as if they were base 10 numbers and convert the result to a base 6 number. Here are some examples of mod 6 subtraction. Note: Θ is the symbol for modulus subtraction:

$$5 \Theta 1 = 4 \mod 6$$
$$18 \Theta 4 = 14 \cong 2(\mod 6)$$

Try the following:

$$15 \Theta 7 = \underline{\hspace{1cm}} \mod 6$$
$$12 \Theta 1 = \underline{\hspace{1cm}} \mod 6$$
$$8 \Theta 10 = \underline{\hspace{1cm}} \mod 6$$

The following table gives the mod 6 addition facts:

+ mod 6	0	1	2	3	4	5
0	0	1	2	3	4	5
1	1	2	3	4	5	0
2	2	3	4	5	0	1
3	3	4	5	0	1	2
4	4	5	0	1	2	3
5	5	0	1	2	3	4

As in base 10, there exists an additive identity in base 6. Recall the following definition:

$$a + 0 = 0 + a = a$$
where a is any real number
and 0 is the additive identity

What is the additive identity for base 6?

Modulus addition and modulus subtraction are only two of the operations that exist for base n numbers. How might you describe modulus 6 multiplication to an absent student? Construct a mod 6 multiplication table similar to the addition table on page 66. Does a multiplicative identity exist in base 6?

ASSIGNMENT: Find the key concepts in the "Mod Squad of 6" lesson. Write each concept on one side of an index card with its definition on the other side. You may have to use other resources to define some terms. Be sure to include all new terms and new symbols.

Frayer Model

±⋯∞≈∈∞∅±⋯∞≈∈∞∅±⋯∅≈∈∞∅±⋯∈≈∈∞∅±⋯±≈∈∞∅±⋯∞≈∈∞∅

WHAT? Description

The Frayer model (Frayer, Frederick, and Klausmeier, 1969) involves word categorization. In this model, students consider the attributes and nonattributes of a concept. A popular version of this model uses a "four-square" graphic: the concept is written in the center of the graphic, and headers are given in each of the four spaces. Students list the definitions, attributes, examples, and nonexamples in the appropriate spaces.

WHY? Objectives

Using the Frayer model, mathematics students will:

- Read closely to search for facts or features of the concept.
- Analyze and write out the attributes and nonattributes of a concept.
- Complete a graphic that may be used as a study aid.

HOW? Example

The example here is for the concept of absolute value equation:

Your Definition	Important Features
$\lvert x \rvert = k$ means that $x = k$ or $x = -k$	$\lvert a \rvert$ means the distance from a to 0 on the number line. $\lvert x \rvert = k$ means that $x = k$ if x is positive and $x = -k$ if k is a negative value
Examples	**Nonexamples**
$\lvert x \rvert = 9$ $x = -9$ and 9 $\lvert x - 1 \rvert = 8$ $x - 1 = 8$ or $x - 1 = -8$ so $x = 9$ or $x = -7$	All absolute value equations must contain the absolute value symbols $\lvert \; \rvert$. The absolute value equation $\lvert x + 1 \rvert = -9$ has no solution since an absolute value cannot be negative.

Frayer Model

NAME _____ DATE _____

$\pm \cdots \infty \approx \in \infty \varnothing \pm \cdots \infty \approx \in \infty \varnothing \pm \cdots \varnothing \approx \in \infty \varnothing \pm \cdots \in \approx \in \infty \varnothing \pm \cdots \pm \approx \in \infty \varnothing \pm \cdots \infty \approx \in \infty \varnothing$

CONCEPT = _____

Your Definition	Important Features
Examples	**Nonexamples**

Question–Answer Relationship (QAR)

WHAT? Description

Question–answer relationship (QAR; Raphael, 1986) is a postreading or reflection strategy. Teachers introduce students to particular types of questions that call for particular answering strategies. There are four levels of questions; two are text based and two are knowledge based. The question types are labeled: *right there, think and search, author and you,* and *on your own.* Raphael suggests giving students a chart, similar to the one in the lesson that follows, that spells out the four question-and-answer strategies.

First, students are taught the four strategies so that they become aware of the relationship between different types of questions and correct responses to these questions. By identifying these differences and using the QAR strategies, students become more skilled at finding the information they need to answer questions on content. To reinforce the strategies, students should be asked to identify the types of questions prior to answering each question.

WHY? Objectives

By using the QAR strategies, the mathematics student will be able to:

- Become aware of and identify different types of questions.
- Hone his or her question-answering skills.
- Explore his or her prior knowledge or opinions on the content.
- Become more efficient and effective at studying content.
- Become better at understanding and responding to questions.

HOW? Examples

The questions that follow refer to "The Secret Society of Pythagoreans: An Ancient Cult" (the reading is on page 78):

Right there: Give three types of figurative numbers.

Think and search: How did Pythagoreans view the concept of number?

Author and you: Would the Pythagoreans be considered a cult in today's world?

On your own: How are cults viewed in today's world?

Question–Answer Relationship (QAR)

NAME _____ DATE _____

$\pm \cdots \infty \approx \in \infty \varnothing \pm \cdots \infty \approx \in \infty \varnothing \pm \cdots \varnothing \approx \in \infty \varnothing \pm \cdots \in \approx \in \infty \varnothing \pm \cdots \pm \approx \in \infty \varnothing \pm \cdots \infty \approx \in \infty \varnothing$

Where are the answers to questions found?

In the text:

Right there: The answer is found in the text. The wording of the question parallels the wording of the answer in the text.

Think and search: The answer is also in the text. However, the question and the answer in the text may be in different words. You will need to think about the ideas in the text and put the answer in your own words.

In your head:

Author and you: The answer is not in the text. You need to put together what the author says with what you think to answer the question.

On your own: The answer is in your head and not in the text. The text should have prompted you to think about the content. Use your background knowledge and insight to answer the question.

Question–Answer Relationship (QAR): Cartesian Coordinate System

NAME _____ DATE _____

± ⋯ ∞ ≈ ∈ ∞ ∅ ± ⋯ ∞ ≈ ∈ ∞ ∅ ± ⋯ ∅ ≈ ∈ ∞ ∅ ± ⋯ ∈ ≈ ∈ ∞ ∅ ± ⋯ ± ≈ ∈ ∞ ∅ ± ⋯ ∞ ≈ ∈ ∞ ∅

René Descartes (pronounced *day cart'*) was a seventeenth-century mathematician and philosopher. It was not unusual for mathematicians in those days to be philosophers, for the invention or discovery of mathematics involved deep thought and intuition. Descartes was believed to have coined the phrase "I think; therefore I am."

Question: How does mathematical invention influence the field of philosophy?

QAR = _____

Answer = _____

_____

_____

Descartes is credited with developing the rectangular coordinate system that we call the Cartesian coordinate system. This system consists of a grid of squares sketched on a plane. The Cartesian coordinate system, also called the rectangular coordinate system or the *xy* plane, contains two perpendicular axes: a vertical line called the *y*-axis and a horizontal line called the *x*-axis.

Question: What are the two axes called in the Cartesian coordinate system?

QAR = _____

Answer = _____

_____

The *origin* is the point at which the two axes meet. Points are plotted in the *xy* plane by locating the point of intersection for the line containing the *x* value and the line containing the *y* value. Ordered pair notation (*x,y*) is used to denote each point. For example, the origin is denoted (0,0).

Question: How would you denote the point that sits at the number 2 on the *x*-axis?

QAR = _____

Answer = _____

Question: Why is the Cartesian coordinate system called the *xy* plane?

QAR = _____

Answer = _____

_____

Postreading Strategies and Activities

Comparison and Contrast Matrix

$\pm\cdots\infty\approx\in\infty\varnothing\pm\cdots\infty\approx\in\infty\varnothing\pm\cdots\varnothing\approx\in\infty\varnothing\pm\cdots\in\approx\in\infty\varnothing\pm\cdots\pm\approx\in\infty\varnothing\pm\cdots\infty\approx\in\infty\varnothing$

WHAT? Description

The comparison and contrast matrix (Vacca and Vacca, 1998) is a matrix that students complete to display similarities and differences between concepts. This activity is similar to semantic feature analysis or the Frayer model; however, the focus here is to compare and contrast features of related concepts. The teacher creates the matrix with key concepts listed across the top of the matrix and features and properties along the left side. Students then complete the matrix by giving the answer to the question posed or writing out the feature asked for.

WHY? Objectives

Completing the comparison and contrast matrix will allow the mathematics student to:

- Reflect on and display the similarities and differences between key mathematical concepts.
- Search for and uncover relevant information from the text.
- Use the matrix for assessment and study purposes.

HOW? Example

The example allows students to compare and contrast three types of equations. The student fills in each square with the features or sketches indicated on the left for each type of equation given along the top of the chart.

Comparison and Contrast Matrix: Equations

	Linear	Quadratic	Cubic
Equation in standard form			
Sketch of basic curve $y = x^n$			
Special characteristics			
Two examples of an equation			

Comparison and Contrast Matrix: Counting Processes

NAME _____   DATE _____

± ·· ∞ ≈ ∈ ∞ ∅ ± ·· ∞ ≈ ∈ ∞ ∅ ± ·· ∅ ≈ ∈ ∞ ∅ ± ·· ∈ ≈ ∈ ∞ ∅ ± ·· ± ≈ ∈ ∞ ∅ ± ·· ∞ ≈ ∈ ∞ ∅

Fill in each square with *yes* if the feature on the left applies to each process along the top or *no* if it does not.

	Fundamental principle of counting	Permutation	Computation
Formula			
Ordered arrangement			
Yields a whole number as a solution			
Uses factorial			

$$\pm \cdots \infty \approx \in \infty \varnothing \pm \cdots \varnothing \approx \in \infty \varnothing$$

Readings in Algebra

Prelude

This chapter consists of three written lessons and one poem. Each piece presents mathematics in a unique manner, ranging from ancient Egyptian multiplication to a mathematical spoof on the true crime of today's world. The first three readings present mathematical content and questions that ask the student to write about the content. These three lessons complement the reading strategies and activities in the preceding chapters.

The final reading is a poem, "True Prime," that uses the language of algebra and calculus to portray images of the underworld of true crime. This poem may be used in the classroom as a springboard for a discussion on the correct and incorrect use of mathematical terms or on the images that mathematical terms might conjure up. All of the readings in this chapter can be used with the reading and writing activities in this book.

Reading 1: The Secret Society of Pythagoreans: An Ancient Cult

$\pm \cdots \infty \approx \in \infty \varnothing \pm \cdots \infty \approx \in \infty \varnothing \pm \cdots \varnothing \approx \in \infty \varnothing \pm \cdots \in \approx \in \infty \varnothing \pm \cdots \pm \approx \in \infty \varnothing \pm \cdots \infty \approx \in \infty \varnothing$

Long before the notion of a cult implied brainwashing and evildoing, there existed a cult or secret society of mathematicians. The leader of this group of mathematical discoverers and inventors was Pythagoras, a Greek mathematician.

The life and times of Pythagoras are steeped in secrecy and myth. Although not much is known about his early life, a few facts do exist. Pythagoras was born somewhere between 580 and 569 B.C. on the Aegean island of Samos. He left Samos at age eighteen to study in Phoenicia and Egypt and wandered as far as Babylonia during the first half-century of his life. Returning to Samos at age fifty, he was immediately banned from his birthplace by hostile political enemies.

Pythagoras settled in Crotonia in southern Italy and founded a school. This was not an uncommon circumstance, as schools were often formed during this time with curricula centering on politics, philosophy, and religion. Approximately three hundred young aristocrats attended Pythagoras's school. The main curriculum consisted of the four subjects of Mathematica called the Quadrivium: Arithmetica (number theory), Geometria (geometry), Harmonia (music), and Astrologia (astronomy). Logic, grammar, and rhetoric were added later, forming the seven liberal arts, which constituted the predominant course of study up through the Middle Ages.

The elite students at Pythagoras's school formed more of a secret society or fraternity than a student body. Because of the secrecy, very little was written, and knowledge was passed to later generations orally. Therefore, many myths and fables have been attributed to the Pythagoreans. Students who entered the school spent three years of listening in silence to the master's lectures before they were initiated into the inner circle. Women were not allowed to attend any of the public lectures because it was long believed that a woman's brain was not created to contain much knowledge and their heads might explode if they became too full! However, Pythagoras did allow approximately twenty-eight women to attend his private lectures.

The Pythagoreans were said to have very curious habits. They re-fused to eat beans, drink wine, pick up fallen objects, or use irons to stir fires. The pentagram (a five-pointed star) was their sign, used to help members of the society recognize each other. This symbol was probably selected because of the many fascinating geometric properties attributed to it. Pythagoreans did not wear wool and refused to kill anything except in sacrifice to the gods. They believed "everything is number," meaning that all of life's mysteries could be explained using positive integers. Legend has it that a former disciple of Pythagoras once acknowledged the existence of an irrational number and was executed by the Pythagoreans. This does seem to go against the Pythagoreans' disdain at the killing of living creatures. The Pythagoreans practiced humility and always ascribed their mathematical discoveries or inventions to their master, Pythagoras.

Pythagoras's death is cloaked in mystery. One story has it that he died in a fire after a violent political revolt. Another has it that his followers formed a human bridge over the fire, allowing him to escape by crawling over their backs. Supposedly, he then fled to a field of beans, and rather than trample the sacred beans, he allowed his enemies to capture and kill him. Long after Pythagoras's death, his followers traveled throughout the world teaching and sharing their mathematical knowledge.

Many mathematical discoveries or inventions are attributed to the Pythagoreans. Several fall under the category of number theory. The Pythagoreans had no consistent number symbols and often used pebbles or dots to denote numbers. They invented the concept of figurative numbers; numbers that form geometric patterns, such as triangular, square or pentagonal numbers.

Consider these triangular and square numbers:

$T_1 = 1$ $T_2 = 3$ $T_3 = 6$ $T_4 = 10$

$S_1 = 1$ $S_2 = 4$ $S_3 = 9$ $S_4 = 16$

The Pythagoreans discovered many properties of these figurative numbers. Note the following relationship:

$T_1 = 1$	$T_2 = 3$	$T_3 = 6$	$T_4 = 10$
$S_1 = 1$	$S_2 = 4$	$S_3 = 9$	$S_4 = 16$
$S_2 = T_1 + T_2$	$S_3 = T_2 + T_3$	$S_4 = T_3 + T_4$	

A geometric proof of this would begin:

$$T_1 +$$
$$T_2 = S_2$$

The formula for finding the nth triangular number is $T_n = \dfrac{n(n+1)}{2}$. Test it!

The formula for finding the nth square number is more straightforward; $S_n = n^2$, which is the area formula for a square.

For all of their curious and mystical beliefs, the secret society of Pythagoreans contributed significantly to the abstract notion of number and the field of mathematics that we call number theory. They also contributed to the fields of philosophy, astronomy, and music. All and all, the Pythagoreans were one of the most productive and inventive cults in history.

Math Problems

1. The first three pentagonal numbers are 1, 5, and 12. Find the fourth pentagonal number.

2. An oblong number could be called a rectangular number. The nth term is given by the formula: $a_n = n(n+1)$.

   Find the fiftieth oblong number. How do you think the formula was developed?

3. In 1665, a French mathematician asserted that every positive integer can be expressed as the sum of three or fewer triangular numbers. Show that this is true for the integers below:

   $16 =$ _____

   $39 =$ _____

   $150 =$ _____

4. Find an integer n such that $t_n = \dfrac{n(n+1)}{2} = 1225$.

Reading 2: Ancient Egyptian Multiplication

Ancient Egypt brings to mind images of massive pyramids and gods with bestial heads. However, one of the greatest accomplishments of the ancient Egyptians was their creation and documentation of one of the first number systems. In fact, the oldest known mathematical documents are two Egyptian papyri that date back to approximately 2000 B.C. These ancient and sacred documents are titled the Rhind Papyrus and the Moscow Mathematical Papyrus. Only pieces of each exist today. The Rhind Papyrus was purchased by A. H. Rhind from the Egyptians in 1858. It was 18 feet long and 13 feet wide. The Moscow Mathematical Papyrus was purchased by the Moscow Museum of Fine Arts in the late 1800s. It was 15 feet long and only 3 inches wide. Both were written in hieratic script, a form of hieroglyphics or picture writing on papyrus reeds.

The introduction to the Rhind Papyrus began with a quotation exemplifying the importance of mathematics to the Egyptians: "Accurate reckoning. The entrance into the knowledge of all existing things and all obscure secrets" (quoted in Katz, 1998, p. 1.)

This papyrus contained various mathematical methods and geometric and counting problems solved using these ancient methods. The number system created and used by the Egyptians as early as 3000 B.C. consisted of symbols representing multiples of 10. The first five symbols were:

1	10	100	1000	10000

This ancient number system was a base 10 and additive system. For example:

$\cap\cap\cap || = 32$

$\cap\cap\cap$ = three tens

$||$ = two ones

Egyptian multiplication was described and used to solve problems in the Rhind Papyrus. The ancient Egyptians used a method of successive doubling, explored in the problem that follows.

PROBLEM: We will consider the problem of multiplying 19 and 21. First, we start with 19: $1 \times 19 = 19$. Then we double both the 1 and the 19, and continue to double:

$\times$	1		19	$\times$
	2		38	
$\times$	4		76	$\times$
	8		152	
$\times$	16		304	$\times$
	21		399	

Note that the numbers in the left column with ×s before them sum up to 21 and their corresponding multiples of 19 sum up to 399, which is the solution to 19×21.

The principle behind the method is quite simple and uses the idea of adding up the partial sums:

1×19 (one 19) = 19

4×19 (four 19s) = 76

16×19 (sixteen 19s)= 304

21×19 (twenty-one 19s) = 399

Now, you try 32×25.

Many of the mathematical methods displayed in the Rhind Papyrus used this idea of decomposing numbers and then recomposing the significant sums. The Chinese use a form of this method called decomposing and recomposing when teaching their children to add and subtract large numbers.

± ⋯ ∞ ≈ ∈ ∞ ∅ ± ⋯ ∞ ≈ ∈ ∞ ∅ ± ⋯ ∅ ≈ ∈ ∞ ∅ ± ⋯ ∈ ≈ ∈ ∞ ∅ ± ⋯ ± ≈ ∈ ∞ ∅ ± ⋯ ∞ ≈ ∈ ∞ ∅

Solving an early Egyptian division problem is really much the same as the multiplication process. See the problem below. However, recall that the actual written form (see the Egyptian numbers above) would look very different.

$624 \div 12$

1	12	
2	24	
4 ×	48	×
8	96	
16 ×	192	×
32 ×	384	×
52	624	

Therefore, the quotient is 52.

Problems

1. Use the Egyptian process to solve the problems below:

   25×46

   $175 \div 25$

   13×51

   $205 \div 4$

2. Can you see why the division process works? How similar to our multiplication and our division are the Egyptian systems?

Reading 3: Marathon Math

± … ∞ ≈ ∈ ∞ ∅ ± … ∞ ≈ ∈ ∞ ∅ ± … ∅ ≈ ∈ ∞ ∅ ± … ∈ ≈ ∈ ∞ ∅ ± … ± ≈ ∈ ∞ ∅ ± … ∞ ≈ ∈ ∞ ∅

Adrian and Sean are in training for the New York Marathon in October. The New York Marathon is a footrace where thousands of participants from all over the world come to run and walk 26.2 miles (approximately 42 kilometers) of New York City streets.

Adrian is an avid runner. She jogs 6 to 8 miles six mornings each week and averages 10- to 11-minute miles. Over the past ten years, Adrian has completed two marathons: one in 5 hours and the other in 4 hours and 35 minutes. Sean is a new runner, starting one year ago. He jogs 4 miles three days each week.

In summer, Adrian designed their training plan. In July through the middle of September, individually Sean and Adrian ran 5 days each week, running 5, 6, 7, and 8 miles, respectively, for four weekdays. On consecutive Saturdays, they ran 10, 13, 16, and 18 miles together. Then, in September, they added two 20-mile runs. Sean was only able to complete the first 20-mile run and quit the second run at 12 miles. For the last two weeks before the marathon, they took it easy and jogged only short runs. (Experienced runners refer to this as the *taper*.)

During training, Adrian collected some data from their runs. The ordered pairs below show distance *(d)* in miles and time *(t)* in minutes *(d,t)*:

> Adrian: (5, 54), (6, 65), (7, 80), (8, 87), (10, 120), (13, 150), (16, 208), (18, 224), (20, 260), (20, 230)
>
> Sean: (5, 60), (6, 72), (7, 88), (8, 100), (10, 120), (13, 150), (16, 208), (18, 224), (20, 260), (12, 144)

Adrian knows that a good time for the New York Marathon is 4 hours. Her goal is to complete the marathon in 4 hours and 15 minutes or less. Sean just hopes to finish the marathon.

What conclusions can you come to regarding the two runners?

- Is training with Sean sabotaging Adrian's training and marathon goals?
- How did you arrive at your conclusion?

± ‥ ∞ ≈ ∈ ∞ ∅ ± ‥ ∞ ≈ ∈ ∞ ∅ ± ‥ ∅ ≈ ∈ ∞ ∅ ± ‥ ∈ ≈ ∈ ∞ ∅ ± ‥ ± ≈ ∈ ∞ ∅ ± ‥ ∞ ≈ ∈ ∞ ∅

Sketch an appropriate graph for this scenario. How does your graph support your conclusions? Write out your answers to the questions above in a clear and coherent paragraph.

Reading 4: True Prime

In the dark invisible crevices of the night
A prime number sleuthed
Searching the lifeless coordinates for clues
To the unsolved, unresolved equation.

Greater than or equal to the task
The prime number trudged on,
Dodging villainous vectors, untangling taloned tangents,
And uncovering uncountable sets.

Into both the positive and negative bounds of the infinite,
The prime number plodded forth.
While exponents powered, derivatives differentiated,
And the integrals disintegrated all about.

But as the first foggy rays of sunrise broke through,
The prime number proved potent.
Unveiled the sinister and silent silhouette
Of the ever-vacuous empty set.

Alas, in the tabloids and periodicals of the dewy morning news,
The prime number was sainted
For discovering and recovering the imaginative
And illusively vacant solution set.

Pat Mower

Part Two

Writing to Learn Algebra

$$\pm \cdots \infty \approx \in \infty \varnothing \pm \cdots \varnothing \approx \in \infty \varnothing$$

Questions that pertain to the foundations of mathematics, although treated by many in recent times, still lack a satisfactory solution. The difficulty has its main source in the ambiguity of language. That is why it is of utmost to examine the very words we use.

Giuseppe Peano, 1889

5

$$\pm \cdots \infty \approx \in \infty \varnothing \pm \cdots \varnothing \approx \in \infty \varnothing$$

Writing to Understand Algebra

Prelude

Writing to Learn as a pedagogical tool arose out of the writing across the curriculum (WAC) movement. Since the early 1980s, WAC advocates have been active in promoting instructional techniques that include writing. Writing to learn mathematics is part of this movement. Many mathematics instructors are very committed to the use of writing for the enhancement of students' comprehension of mathematical concepts and processes.

The writing process includes research, reflection, analysis, synthesis, rewriting, and communicating; many of these skills are equally valuable for learning mathematics. The cognitive processes required in the writing process cause students to think before they proceed to use algorithms or solve problems. Often, problem solving in mathematics can become a mechanical process in which the student may learn how to do it but not why it works. Writing encourages students to think beyond the algorithm and consider why each step logically follows the step before it.

The writing-to-learn strategies and activities in this chapter speak to why algorithms work, encourage student reflection, demand analysis of mathematical processes, and require students to explore and discover the fine points of and logic behind the mathematics. These activities are usually read and assessed by the teacher.

Kiniry and Rose (1990) suggest the following writing-to-learn strategies: defining, serializing, classifying, summarizing, comparing, and analyzing. Other important writing-to-learn strategies are narrating, paraphrasing, detailing, recounting, illustrating, depicting, and characterizing. This chapter contains the following activities that address many of these strategies:

Section	Strategies Addressed
In Your Own Words: A Paraphrasing Activity	Defining, summarizing, depicting, illustrating
MO (Method of Operation)	Defining, analyzing, detailing, illustrating
Graph Description Activity	Detailing, illustrating, analyzing
Crib Sheets	Summarizing, paraphrasing, detailing
Math Story Activity	Narrating, recounting
Math Ads	Analyzing, illustrating, characterizing
The Writing Is on the Wall	Defining, classifying
Creating a Math Mnemonic	Characterizing, summarizing, analyzing
Creation of Written Problems (or Fat Men in Pink Leotards)	Narrating, analyzing
Math Concept Paragraphs	Summarizing, analyzing
Math Biographies	Characterizing, narrating
Experimenting to Learn Algebra Reports	Recounting, serializing
Concept Math	Illustrating, characterizing
Learning Logs	Summarizing, categorizing

In Your Own Words: A Paraphrasing Activity

WHAT? Description

One of the most common excuses that students give for not reading the text is that they do not understand the language of the text. The paraphrasing activity helps students to target and interpret the key concepts of the text. By rewriting portions of the text, the students demystify and make personal meaning of mathematical content.

Students are assigned small portions of the text to read and translate into their own words. This activity works equally well with concept definitions, theorems, and examples. Having students read their translations to each other allows student writers to consider different interpretations and pinpoint misconceptions. If the translations are handed in, the teacher can correct faulty thinking.

WHY? Objectives

The paraphrasing activity encourages algebra students to:

- Read the text.
- Examine content closely and ask questions when necessary.
- Gain ownership of algebra by translating it into language that makes sense and is relevant to their own life.
- Consider peers' interpretations of the content.
- Identify misconceptions.

HOW? Examples

See the examples in the lessons that follow.

In Your Own Words: A Paraphrasing Activity

NAME _____   DATE _____

ASSIGNMENT: Read the passage that follows. Then write out your definition of a vertical asymptote. Be clear, and use at least two complete sentences. Be prepared to share your definition with your peers. You may use other sources to help develop your definition.

Vertical Asymptote: A *vertical asymptote* is a vertical line such that the graph of a function gets very close to but never touches. In other words, as x approaches the line $x = c$ (the vertical asymptote), the graph of f will go to positive or negative infinity. For example, let

$$f(x) = \frac{3}{x-1}$$

Consider the following table of points on the graph:

x	y
.9	−30
.99	−300
.999	−3000
1.1	30
1.01	300
1.001	3000

Note that as x gets close to 1 from the left or in values less than 1, f gets smaller and smaller:

As $x \to 1^-$, $y \to -\infty$

Also, as x gets close to 1 from the right, f gets larger and larger:

As $x \to 1^+$, $y \to +\infty$

In the following graph of f, the dashed vertical line represents the vertical asymptote:

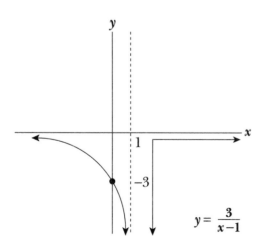

$$y = \frac{3}{x-1}$$

In Your Own Words: A Paraphrasing Activity

NAME _____ DATE _____

± ··· ∞ ≈ ∈ ∞ ∅ ± ··· ∞ ≈ ∈ ∞ ∅ ± ··· ∅ ≈ ∈ ∞ ∅ ± ··· ∈ ≈ ∈ ∞ ∅ ± ··· ± ≈ ∈ ∞ ∅ ± ··· ∞ ≈ ∈ ∞ ∅

Complex Numbers

ASSIGNMENT: Read the section in the text on complex numbers. Then paraphrase the section describing complex numbers, writing as if you were writing or talking to a student who was absent the day we covered complex numbers. Be clear, and address the following items in your description:

- What is a complex number?
- What does a complex number look like?
- How is a complex number like or unlike a real number?
- Give an example of a complex number that is not a real number.

A complex number is a _____

_____

_____

_____

_____

_____

_____

_____

_____

Writing to Understand Algebra   **95**

MO (Method of Operation)

$\pm \cdots \infty \approx \in \infty \emptyset \pm \cdots \infty \approx \in \infty \emptyset \pm \cdots \emptyset \approx \in \infty \emptyset \pm \cdots \in \approx \in \infty \emptyset \pm \cdots \pm \approx \in \infty \emptyset \pm \cdots \infty \approx \in \infty \emptyset$

WHAT? Description

Much of mathematical content consists of processes. Students need to know the "how-to's" or methods for simplifying or arriving at solutions. Having students write out processes (methods of operation) reinforces their understanding of how to solve problems and helps them to consider the fine points of or exceptions to the rule. If we consider the text or the classroom to be the scene of the crime and the problems to be the criminals, then the problem-solving processes are the modus operandi, or the MOs, for problem solving.

Students might be asked to write out the MO for solving a linear equation, $ax + b = 0$, or the MO for factoring the difference of two squares. Asking the student to write out the MO as if he or she were talking to a student who is just learning this process encourages the writer to be clear and complete.

WHY? Objectives

The creation of an MO encourages the algebra student to:

- Reflect on and learn the process in question.
- Consider the details and exceptions to the rule for the process.
- Take time and thought to consider the audience and clarify writing accordingly.

HOW? Examples

Here are some examples of assignments:

- Write out the MO for solving the linear equation $ax + b = 0$ for a student who missed this lesson. Consider a and b to be positive real numbers.

- Write out the MO for finding the inverse function f^{-1} of a one-to-one function f.
- Fill in the blank steps for solving the quadratic equation below. Consider c to be a positive real number. Then write out the MO in your own words:

$x^2 - c = 0$

1. _____

2. _____

3. _____

Your MO: _____

_____

Here is an example of a student MO:

MO for solving $ax + b = c$ [a,b,c are real numbers]

1. Subtract b from both sides, giving $ax = c - b$

2. Divide both sides by a, giving $\dfrac{(c-b)}{a}$

3. Compute and give the solution: $x = \dfrac{(c-b)}{a}$

MO (Method of Operation): Simplifying a Complex Fraction

NAME _____ DATE _____

$$\pm \cdots \infty \approx \in \infty \varnothing \pm \cdots \infty \approx \in \infty \varnothing \pm \cdots \varnothing \approx \in \infty \varnothing \pm \cdots \in \approx \in \infty \varnothing \pm \cdots \pm \approx \in \infty \varnothing \pm \cdots \infty \approx \in \infty \varnothing$$

Consider the fraction:

$$\frac{2-3i}{1+2i}$$

Write out the steps for simplifying this complex fraction. Recall that the resulting fraction must be in simplest form and the denominator must not contain any imaginary parts:

1. _____

2. _____

3. _____

4. _____

5. _____

6. _____

Now consider the following general form of a complex fraction:

$$\frac{a+bi}{c+di}$$

Write out the steps for simplifying this general complex fraction. Recall that the resulting fraction must be in simplest form and the denominator must not contain any imaginary parts:

1. _____

2. _____

3. _____

4. _____

5. _____

6. _____

Algebra Out Loud

MO (Method of Operation): Factoring MOs

Write out the steps for factoring the difference of two squares:

$$x^2 - b^2$$

1. _____

2. _____

3. _____

4. _____

Write out the steps for factoring a perfect square quadratic:

$$x^2 + 4x + 4 \qquad or \qquad x^2 + 2x + 1$$

1. _____

2. _____

3. _____

4. _____

5. _____

One thing I discovered about factoring in general is

_____

_____

_____

_____

Graph Description Activity

WHAT? Description

The graph description activity encourages students to reflect on and choose appropriate terms to describe the specific features of a graph. First, the teacher sketches two graphs and makes copies for each student. The students are divided into two groups of equal size. Each student in each group is given a copy of one of the graphs to observe and write a description of on a separate sheet of paper. The descriptions are then traded with the members of the opposite group. Each student attempts to sketch the graph based on the written description he or she receives. The original version of the graph is then viewed, and students are encouraged to discuss their descriptions and sketches.

WHY? Objectives

The graph description activity allows mathematics students to:

- Review and reflect on appropriate graph descriptors.
- Consider their audience's knowledge before writing and choose appropriate language.
- Read carefully when preparing to sketch their graph.
- Build their graphing vocabulary.
- Assess their knowledge of graphing vocabulary.

HOW? Examples

The examples that follow are of three student descriptions of the same graph:

Student A: The wavy line starts at the point zero,zero and rises (going horizontally) to a +3 on the *y*-axis, then falling on the *x*-axis to a positive two on the *x*-axis, then back up to positive four and suddenly goes straight (horizontally) when it hits a 3.

Student B: Draw a snakelike line (on the right side of the graph) starting at zero, with the top of the first curve up to 3 on the *y*-axis, back down to 2 on the *x*-axis, continuing down to make another curve. Bring it back up to 4 on the same line, continue up to 3 again (on *y*) and straight out to the right with an arrow.

Student C: The graph starts at 0,0 and curves up to 1,3. It then curves down crossing at 2,0 and continues down to 3, −3. It then curves down crossing at 2,0 and continues up to 4,3. This should look similar to a sine wave. It then continues to run parallel to the *x*-axis at a height of 3.

Here is the actual graph:

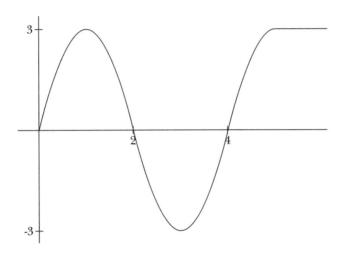

Graph Description Activity

ASSIGNMENT: Consider the graph shown here. On the lines below, write out a description of it. Choose your vocabulary carefully so that another student can use your written description to sketch the graph.

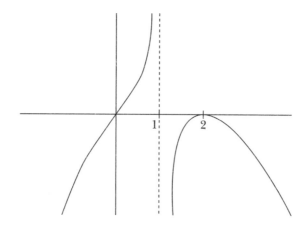

_____

_____

_____

_____

_____

_____

_____

_____

_____

Graph Description Activity

NAME _____   DATE _____

± ··· ∞ ≈ ∈ ∞ ∅ ± ··· ∞ ≈ ∈ ∞ ∅ ± ··· ∅ ≈ ∈ ∞ ∅ ± ··· ∈ ≈ ∈ ∞ ∅ ± ··· ± ≈ ∈ ∞ ∅ ± ··· ∞ ≈ ∈ ∞ ∅

ASSIGNMENT: Consider the graph shown here. On the lines below, write out a description of the graph in words. Choose your vocabulary carefully so that another student can use your written description to sketch the graph.

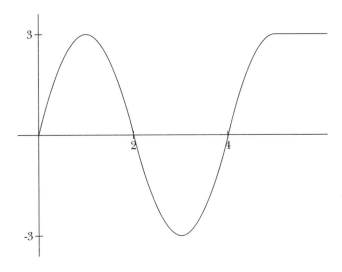

_____

_____

_____

_____

_____

_____

_____

_____

Crib Sheets

WHAT? Description

The creation of a crib sheet is an excellent study strategy for students preparing for an exam. The crib sheet is a one-page document containing the important information from a particular chapter, a section of the mathematics text, or related class discussions and lectures. Each student must select and summarize the key concepts, along with definitions, theorems, features, and examples. Each student's crib sheet will be unique, containing content and examples that make sense to that particular student. Teachers decide whether students are to use crib sheets during quizzes or exams. Regarding the crib sheet, students often say that the creation of the crib sheet is one of the best study methods they have used.

The crib sheet format may be predetermined or left up to the student to create. We consider two different formats here.

WHY? Objectives

The creation of a crib sheet gives the mathematics student the opportunity to:

- Choose the key concepts from the text and classroom instruction.
- Review and summarize the content to be assessed.
- Develop a better study technique.
- Target areas where he or she needs more review or practice.
- Search for and work out appropriate examples of problems.

A Partial Example of a Crib Sheet on Descriptive Statistics

Section	Concept	Description/Notes	Example
Measures of central tendency	Mean	Value determined by adding all values and dividing this sum by the number of values in a data set	Data = 1,4,4,5,6 $\text{Mean} = \dfrac{1+4+4+5+6}{5} = \dfrac{20}{5} = 4$
Measures of central tendency	Median	Middlemost value of a data set	Data = 1,4,4,5,6 Median = 4
Measures of central tendency	Mode	Most recurring value of a data set	Data = 1,4,4,5,6 Mode = 4
Measures of spread	Range	Maximum value − minimum value	Data = 1,4,4,5,6 Range = 6 − 1 = 5
Measures of spread	Standard deviation	Square root of the mean of the squares of the differences between each data value and the mean	Square root of $\left(\dfrac{(1-4)^2 + (4-4)^2 + (4-4)^2 + (5-4)^2 + (6-4)^2}{5} \right)$ ≈ 1.67

Crib Sheets

NAME _____ DATE _____

± ∞ ≈ ∈ ∞ ∅ ± ∞ ≈ ∈ ∞ ∅ ± ∅ ≈ ∈ ∞ ∅ ± ∈ ≈ ∈ ∞ ∅ ± ± ≈ ∈ ∞ ∅ ± ∞ ≈ ∈ ∞ ∅

Fill in the following table with content that will help you prepare for the upcoming exam. Use language that makes sense to you.

Section	Concept	Description	Example	Notes/Facts

Crib Sheets

NAME _____   DATE _____

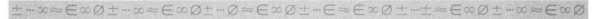

Review the chapter and your class notes to find all key concepts and processes. Then fill the back of this sheet with all vital content (that is, content you anticipate will be on the exam). List all definitions, methods of operation, and examples in a manner that makes sense to you and that will help you prepare for this exam.

Example of student-created crib sheet:

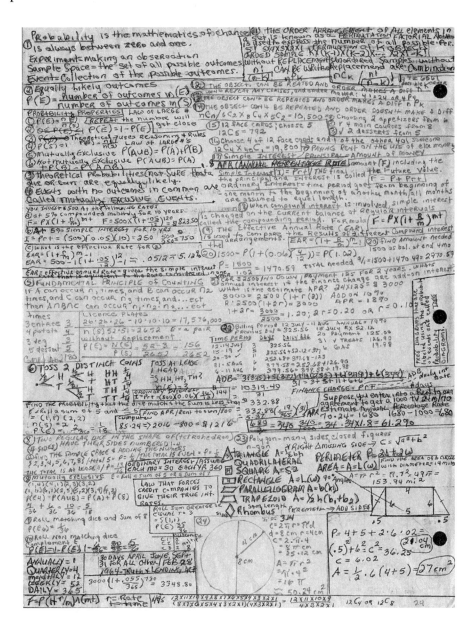

Math Story Activity

WHAT? Description

During the math story activity, students are given a list of mathematical terms or concepts and asked to use all of the terms correctly to create a short story. This activity may be used during or after the lesson containing the specified terms. Asking students to use mathematics terms or concepts to create stories requires that they learn the meaning of these terms.

Student writers are encouraged to be creative but also to pay close attention to the meanings of the mathematical terms. The stories may be fiction or nonfiction; witty, silly, sad, or dramatic. However, students should be given some guidelines to follow when creating their stories. Being explicit about what constitutes an A paper is equally important to the student writer and the teacher reader/grader.

WHY? Objectives

The math story activity encourages the mathematics student to:

- Learn the meanings of specified terms.
- Consider the appropriate use of mathematics terms in writing.
- Be creative and demonstrate this creativity.
- Consider the aesthetic quality of mathematics.

HOW? Assignment Criteria

Follow these directions to earn full credit:

1. Your story must contain all listed terms.
2. Each term must be used correctly. Use the text or dictionary to check on definitions and correct use of terms. You may be creative with each term, but in at least one place, use the term correctly or in a manner that clearly demonstrates what it means.
3. Your story may be fiction or nonfiction.
4. Your story should contain an introduction and a conclusion and follow a logical story line.
5. Your story must be at least one page but no more than two pages.
6. Be creative, and choose a theme that has relevance to you.

Math Story Activity

NAME _____ DATE _____

$\pm \cdots \infty \approx \in \infty \varnothing \pm \cdots \infty \approx \in \infty \varnothing \pm \cdots \varnothing \approx \in \infty \varnothing \pm \cdots \in \approx \in \infty \varnothing \pm \cdots \pm \approx \in \infty \varnothing \pm \cdots \infty \approx \in \infty \varnothing$

ASSIGNMENT: Use the following terms to create a short story:

> graph
> line
> slope
> x intercept
> y intercept
> parallel
> perpendicular
> vertical line
> horizontal line

Follow these directions to earn full credit:

1. Your story must contain all listed terms.
2. Each term must be used correctly. Use the text or dictionary to check on definitions and correct use of terms. You may be creative with each term, but in at least one place, use the term correctly or in a manner that clearly demonstrates what it means.
3. Your story may be fiction or nonfiction.
4. Your story should contain an introduction and a conclusion and follow a logical story line.
5. Your story must be at least one page but no more than two pages.
6. Be creative, and choose a theme that has relevance to you.

Math Story Activity: Logarithms

NAME _____ DATE _____

$\pm\cdots\infty\approx\in\infty\emptyset\pm\cdots\infty\approx\in\infty\emptyset\pm\cdots\emptyset\approx\in\infty\emptyset\pm\cdots\in\approx\in\infty\emptyset\pm\cdots\pm\approx\in\infty\emptyset\pm\cdots\infty\approx\in\infty\emptyset$

ASSIGNMENT: Use the following terms to create a short story:

> logarithm
> base
> argument
> power
> natural log
> common log
> ln
> e
> inverse
> product rule
> quotient rule
> power rule

Use the following terms to create a short story. Follow the directions below to earn full credit:

1. Your story must contain all listed terms.

2. Each term must be used correctly. Use the text or dictionary to check on definitions and correct use of terms. You may be creative with each term, but in at least one place, use the term correctly or in a manner that clearly demonstrates what the term means.

3. Your story may be fiction or nonfiction.

4. Your story should contain an introduction and a conclusion and follow a logical story line.

5. Your story must be at least one page but no more than two pages.

6. Be creative, and choose a theme that has relevance to you.

I'm a natural Log!

Math Story Activity

± ⋯ ∞ ≈ ∈ ∞ ∅ ± ⋯ ∞ ≈ ∈ ∞ ∅ ± ⋯ ∅ ≈ ∈ ∞ ∅ ± ⋯ ∈ ≈ ∈ ∞ ∅ ± ⋯ ± ≈ ∈ ∞ ∅ ± ⋯ ∞ ≈ ∈ ∞ ∅

ASSIGNMENT: Use the following terms to create a short story:

> rational equation
> intercept
> asymptote
> vertical
> horizontal
> maximum
> minimum
> zero

Follow these directions to earn full credit:

1. Your story must contain all listed terms.

2. Each term must be used correctly. Use the text or dictionary to check on definitions and correct use of terms. You may be creative with each term, but in at least one place, use the term correctly or in a manner that clearly demonstrates what the term means.

3. Your story may be fiction or nonfiction.

4. Your story should contain an introduction and a conclusion and follow a logical story line.

5. Your story must be at least one page but no more than two pages.

6. Be creative, and choose a theme that has relevance to you.

Math Ads

WHAT? Description

Having students write advertisements for mathematical concepts is an excellent way to encourage them to research these topics. Students become salespersons or promoters for their chosen concepts. To be effective salespersons, students must become experts on their products. They must sell the audience on the usefulness, uniqueness, and beauty of their mathematical concepts.

During this activity, students should have access to several resources containing the appropriate content. Students will learn to research mathematical topics as they are introduced to different interpretations of these topics. Students then collect and adapt this information into a format fitting to an advertisement.

Here are some tips for this activity:

- Present students with multiple resources.
- Show students an example of what you consider a good ad.
- Encourage students to be creative.

WHY? Objectives

The creation of a mathematical advertisement allows the student the opportunity to:

- Research a mathematical concept of her or his choosing.
- Read different interpretations of the concept in question.
- Think deeply about the chosen concept.
- See and present mathematics in a new light.

HOW? Examples

Several examples of good ads for math concepts follow.

Slope $25

$$m = \frac{\Delta y}{\Delta x}$$

Get the latest slant on your line!

Now on Sale

A formula for all inclines!

Use it

⇒for hills, ramps, and ladders!

⇒to descend or ascend!

⇒to graph lines!

⇒to develop linear equations!

Added advantage: it can easily be transformed to the point slope form of a linear equation.

Be it positive or negative, the slope will determine your lines.

Now available at a coordinate plane near you!

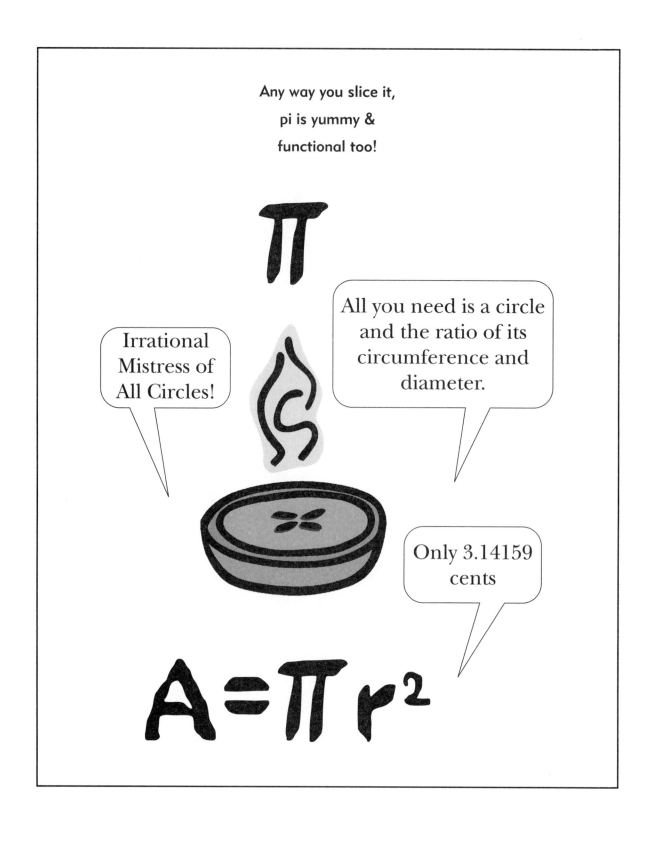

OPEN YOUR MIND

UNLIMITED POSSIBILITIES

$$\frac{-b \pm \sqrt{b^2 - 4ac}}{2a}$$

QUADRATIC FORMULA

THE FORMULA IS NOT DISCRIMINANT,
ANYBODY CAN USE IT
SOLVE UNLIMITED QUADRATIC EQUATIONS AND
FIND ACTUAL REAL SOLUTIONS
FORMULA WORKS WELL WITH OTHERS

WARNING:
IMAGINARY SOLUTIONS POSSIBLE

IT IS NOT A HALLUCINATION

The Writing Is on the Wall

WHAT? Description

Elementary teachers often use a word wall or bulletin board to post new words to help students learn their spelling and vocabulary. A more sophisticated version of the word wall is the posting of the Top Ten, Fabulous Five, or Foremost Four mathematics concepts from each lesson or chapter on a bulletin board or poster board. Students should be asked to give the key concepts, and the definition and hierarchy of the terms should be discussed.

The most significant mathematical concepts and terms are collected by students and used to construct glossaries, which are lists of words with their definitions. Students in this way become wordsmiths. Students might be allowed to use their glossaries during special quizzes or exams or for studying for exams.

WHY? Objectives

The creation of a math glossary allows mathematics students to:

- Consider and select the key concepts from the text or lesson.
- Construct a study aid for preparing for exams.
- Make personal meaning of concepts by writing out definitions in their own words.

HOW? Examples

Here are some examples of posters.

Fabulous Five Terms from a Lesson on Prime Numbers

Prime

Composite

Factor

Divisible

Multiple

Top Ten Concepts from a Lesson on Graphing a Quadratic Function

Quadratic	x intercept
Parabola	y intercept
Vertex	Axis of Symmetry
Maximum	Leading Coefficient
Minimum	Constant

Creating a Math Mnemonic

WHAT? Description

Mnemonics are devices such as rhymes used as memory aids. One example of a mnemonic is an acronym or a word formed from the first letters or parts of words. A popular mnemonic is the phrase "Please Excuse My Dear Aunt Sally," an aid for memorizing the order of operations: P stands for parentheses, E for exponents, M for multiplication, D for division, A for addition, and S for subtraction. Although memorizing is only one of the many strategies for learning mathematics, it is nonetheless vital to the learning of certain problem-solving processes.

This activity works very well when the lesson involves a sequential process, such as the graphing of a parabola. First, the process is demonstrated. Then the students work together or separately to create mnemonics to assist in their memorization of the steps of the process. The mnemonic might be an acronym, a rhyme, a rap song, or any other catchy wording that is easily remembered.

WHY? Objectives

The creation of a mnemonic:

- Reinforces the learning of the steps of a mathematical process.
- Allows students to bring personal meaning to mathematics.
- Allows students to easily recall the steps of a process.

HOW? Examples

The lessons that follow are examples of assignments.

Creating a Math Mnemonic: Graphing a Quadratic Function

NAME _____   DATE _____

ASSIGNMENT: Use the process to help create a mnemonic to aid you in remembering how to graph any quadratic function.

Consider the quadratic function:

$$y = x^2 + 2x - 24$$

Sketch the graph of y.

1. Find the vertex, which is a maximum or minimum of the function.
   If $y = ax^2 + bx + c$

   $$x = \frac{-b}{2a} = \frac{-2}{2(1)} = -1$$

   $$f(-1) = 1 - 2 - 24 = -25$$

   Vertex = $(-1, -25)$

   Use the letter V or Max or Min.

2. Decide if the graph opens upward or downward. Rule: if $a > 0$, then the parabola opens up.

   Use the words UP or DOWN.

3. Find the y intercept. When $x = 0$, then $y = 24$.
   y intercept = $(0, 24)$

   Use the letter I for intercepts.

4. Find x intercept(s).
   When $y = 0$, find x.
   $$0 = x^2 + 2x - 24 = (x - 6)(x + 4)$$
   $x = 6$ and -4

5. Sketch the graph.

   Use either the letter G or S.

   Here are some possible mnemonics that result from this activity:

   Max Up, It's Super!
   Max, Min, Up, Down, It's a Snap!
   Max Up, Min Down, It's the Graph!

Creating a Math Mnemonic: The Process for Adding Two Fractions

NAME _____   DATE _____

1. Find the LCD for the denominators.   LCD or L

2. Transform or change each fraction to an   T
   equivalent fraction with the new common
   denominator.

3. Rewrite the two fractions as one fraction   R or W
   by adding the two numerators and placing
   the sum over the common denominator.

4. Simplify the resulting fraction.   S

   Here are some possible mnemonics that result from this activity:

   Leave The Rest to uS
   Love Those Rap Songs
   Least Common Denominator Takes us to the Right Solution

   Try writing your own mnemonic:

   _____

   _____

Creating a Math Mnemonic

NAME _____ DATE _____

± ⋯ ∞ ≈ ∈ ∞ ∅ ± ⋯ ∞ ≈ ∈ ∞ ∅ ± ⋯ ∅ ≈ ∈ ∞ ∅ ± ⋯ ∈ ≈ ∈ ∞ ∅ ± ⋯ ± ≈ ∈ ∞ ∅ ± ⋯ ∞ ≈ ∈ ∞ ∅

ASSIGNMENT: Use the factoring process to create a mnemonic.

Solve a quadratic equation by factoring:

1. Set the equation equal to zero.

2. Factor.

3. Set each linear factor equal to zero.

4. Solve each linear equation.

5. Check the solution in the original equation.

Mnemonic: _____

_____

Creation of Written Problems
(or Fat Men in Pink Leotards)

± … ∞ ≈ ∈ ∝ ∅ ± … ∞ ≈ ∈ ∞ ∅ ± … ∅ ≈ ∈ ∝ ∅ ± … ∈ ≈ ∈ ∞ ∅ ± … ± ≈ ∈ ∞ ∅ ± … ∞ ≈ ∈ ∞ ∅

WHAT? Description

Many algebra students find solving word problems difficult and confusing. This activity asks them to create their own applications, which allows them to look at solving written problems from a different angle. Students do best with this activity when the mathematical content is specific, such as solving problems through the use of two equations and two unknowns.

Students work in pairs or small groups of three or four to create the problem. The groups then exchange problems and work solutions out on the board.

WHY? Objectives

The creation of written problems allows the algebra student to:

- Look closely at text problems.
- Think creatively and consider the word problem from the writer's angle.
- Work out the numbers first to find solutions that work and that are easy to work with, such as integers.
- Understand why, and not just how, the solution process works.

HOW? Examples

The following examples of student-generated problems use one equation and one variable (Mower, 1995):

> Baby Sumba and Mufassa leave the cave at the same time, but in opposite directions. If Sumba runs at 4 mph and Mufassa runs at 10 mph, how long will it take for them to be 24 miles apart?

The FMIPL (Fat Men in Pink Leotards) is holding its seventh annual "Skip-a-thon" tomorrow. If Gorgio skips at an average of 5 mph and Frank skips at an average of 2 mph, how long will Gorgio have to wait for Frank at the end of the 45-mile race?

A person once had some blue fish and some green fish, for a total of 500 fish. Each blue fish weighed 1.5 pounds and each green fish weighed 3 pounds, so he had a total of 1,500 pounds of fish. After he went on vacation and forgot to feed them, how many blue fish and green fish did he have left?

STUDENT REALIZATION

1. You must work backward to get the numbers to work out nicely.

2. You must assume an ideal mathematical world where the wind does not blow and fish do not die from starvation.

3. You must understand why the problem works and not just how.

Math Concept Paragraphs

WHAT? Description

In a concept paragraph, the student describes a mathematical concept or a feature of the concept using as many mathematical terms as possible. Prior to the assignment of the concept paragraph, the teacher and students should review the rudiments of the concept paragraph:

- An introductory thesis statement that introduces the concept
- One to three sentences about the thesis sentence that describe the features or characteristics of the concept

Students might be encouraged to use as many mathematical terms as possible if they are awarded points for each term they use. This assignment may be enhanced by asking the student to include an example of the concept alluded to in the paragraph. The example might be an equation, graph, numerical process, or sketch.

WHY? Objectives

The student writer of a concept paragraph will learn:

- How to compose a clear concept paragraph.
- The features and characteristics of the concept.
- How to communicate using the vocabulary of algebra.
- How to transfer mathematical content into her or his own words.

HOW? Examples

The following algebraic concepts could be used for concept paragraphs:

function

domain

range

slope

ordered pair

parabola

composition

inverse function

Here is an example of a good concept paragraph:

A slope is the numerical measure of the slant of a line in the xy plane. The value of the slope is found by using two points on the line and finding the quotient of the difference between the y values divided by the difference between the x values. A positive value for the slope means the line ascends, and a negative value means the line descends from left to right. A slope of 0 means the line is horizontal, and an undefined slope means the line is vertical.

Math Concept Paragraphs

NAME _____ DATE _____

$\pm \cdots \infty \approx \in \infty \varnothing \pm \cdots \infty \approx \in \infty \varnothing \pm \cdots \varnothing \approx \in \infty \varnothing \pm \cdots \in \approx \in \infty \varnothing \pm \cdots \pm \approx \in \infty \varnothing \pm \cdots \infty \approx \in \infty \varnothing$

ASSIGNMENT: Write a concept paragraph about one of the key concepts from this chapter.

Guidelines

Each concept paragraph must contain the following:

- An introductory thesis statement that introduces the concept
- Two to three sentences that describe features or characteristics of the concept
- At least ten mathematical terms
- Complete, clear sentences

Grading

Each paragraph is worth _____ points, according to the following criteria:

Thesis statement is clear and accurate.	_____ points
At least ten math terms are used.	_____ points
The paragraph contains two to three clear and accurate sentences describing features.	_____ points
The mechanics, grammar, and spelling are correct.	_____ points

Example

A slope is the numerical measure of the slant of a line in the xy plane. The value of the slope is found by using two points on the line and finding the quotient of the difference between the y values divided by the difference between the x values. A positive value for the slope means the line ascends, and a negative value means the line descends from left to right. A slope of 0 means the line is horizontal, and an undefined slope means the line is vertical.

Algebra Out Loud

Math Biographies

$\pm \cdots \infty \approx \in \infty \varnothing \pm \cdots \infty \approx \in \infty \varnothing \pm \cdots \varnothing \approx \in \infty \varnothing \pm \cdots \in \approx \in \infty \varnothing \pm \cdots \pm \approx \in \infty \varnothing \pm \cdots \infty \approx \in \infty \varnothing$

WHAT? Description

One way to understand algebra is to explore how it came to be. Several ancient men contributed to the development of the field of mathematics called algebra. In fact, the word *algebrista* in early Spain meant bonesetting. Often, the setting of bones in Spain took place at the neighborhood barbershop and included the processes of reduction and reunion. At the same time, the Arabs considered the term *al-jabr* to mean reunion. The term *jabr* came to mean the restoring or reunion of bones. The Arabs contributed significantly to the development of algebra as a field of mathematics. However, no one man or woman could be considered the inventor or discoverer of algebra; this development, like the creation of many other branches of mathematics, was a step-by-step process, where one invention led to another.

A biography is the write-up of a person's life story. The research, writing, and sharing of a biography of a mathematician who contributed to the development of algebra helps students to consider how and why the field of algebra arose.

The assignment of a biography of a mathematician should include the format for the write-up. For example, each biography might consist of the following parts:

- Early life
- Education and career
- Family or social life
- Algebraic contributions
- Later life

WHY? Objectives

The creation of a math biography allows the algebra student to:

- See the step-by-step development of algebra.
- Consider how and why the field of algebra arose.
- Explore the early need for algebraic processes.
- Consider whether algebra was invented or discovered.

Math Biographies

±⋯∞≈∈∞∅±⋯∞≈∈∞∅±⋯∅≈∈∞∅±⋯∈≈∈∞∅±⋯±≈∈∞∅±⋯∞≈∈∞∅

ASSIGNMENT: Write a four- to five-page biography of one of the following mathematicians: Al-Khowárizmi, Abu Kamil, Omar Knayyam, Liu Hui, Diophantus, or Fibonacci.

Guidelines

1. Each biography must contain the following parts of your mathematician's life:

    Early life
    Education and career
    Family or social life
    Algebraic contributions
    Later life
    Resource list

2. Use at least three different sources, with one from the library.
3. The biography must be word-processed.
4. It should be a minimum of four pages and maximum of six pages in length.
5. The last page should be a bibliography.
6. Address your mathematician's influence on the field of algebra.

Math Biographies (continued)

$\pm \cdots \infty \approx \in \infty \varnothing \pm \cdots \infty \approx \in \infty \varnothing \pm \cdots \varnothing \approx \in \infty \varnothing \pm \cdots \in \approx \in \infty \varnothing \pm \cdots \pm \approx \in \infty \varnothing \pm \cdots \infty \approx \in \infty \varnothing$

Grading

Content score = _____

    Contains all required parts?

    Contains accurate information?

Mechanics score = _____

    Grammar, spelling, clarity, transitions, introduction, conclusion?

    Follows guidelines?

Resources score = _____

    Format?

    Number of sources used?

Final grade = _____

Experimenting-to-Learn-Algebra Reports

± … ∞ ≈ ∈ ∞ ∅ ± … ∞ ≈ ∈ ∞ ∅ ± … ∅ ≈ ∈ ∞ ∅ ± … ∈ ≈ ∈ ∞ ∅ ± … ± ≈ ∈ ∞ ∅ ± … ∞ ≈ ∈ ∞ ∅

WHAT? Description

The National Council of Supervisors of Mathematics (1988), which writes, "Algebra is the language through which most of mathematics is communicated" (p. 150), recommends that the learning of algebra begin in elementary school with children solving problems like $7 + ? = 10$ and recognizing letters in perimeter and area formulas. By the time students encounter an actual algebra course, they should have had many prealgebraic learning experiences—experiences that reinforce the notion that algebra is the generalization of problem solving. Algebra experiments are an extension of this learning process.

An algebra experiment may involve paper folding, ball tossing, or other hands-on activities. Students may use graphing calculators, computer programs, or more low-tech materials such as stopwatches and rulers. The point of the algebra experiment is to encourage students to reach conjectures or conclusions regarding the experiment or, in some cases, find general equations that represent the experiment's outcomes. Students then should be required to communicate their findings. The experiment's write-up is similar to employees' reports to colleagues or customers in the real world.

The format of the write-up should be well laid out for the student. A fill-in-the-blanks form is the one way to encourage consistency and completeness.

WHY? Objectives

The writing of the experiment report allows the student to:

- Experiment with hands-on mathematical projects.
- Form conjectures or reach conclusions regarding these experiments.
- Communicate algebraic experiences.
- Practice writing technological reports.

HOW? Examples

The following lessons provide examples.

Experimenting-to-Learn-Algebra Reports: Paper Folding: How Thick Can We Get?

NAME _____   DATE _____

± ⋯ ∞ ≈ ∈ ∞ ∅ ± ⋯ ∞ ≈ ∈ ∞ ∅ ± ⋯ ∅ ≈ ∈ ∞ ∅ ± ⋯ ∈ ≈ ∈ ∞ ∅ ± ⋯ ± ≈ ∈ ∞ ∅ ± ⋯ ∞ ≈ ∈ ∞ ∅

Materials

One sheet of typing paper
Pencil and paper for recording
Graphing calculator with list capabilities
Manual for calculator

Experiment

1. A piece of typing paper is approximately .0032 inch thick. You will be folding the paper and measuring the thickness in inches. For each fold, fill in the table on the next page, using column 1 for the number of folds and column 2 for the thickness of the folded paper.
2. Also for each fold, input the number of folds in L1 and the thickness of folded paper in L2 in the calculator.
3. To begin the experiment, fold the paper in half. How thick is it? Record the thickness on paper and in the calculator.
4. Fold the paper again. How thick is it now? Record the thickness on paper and in the calculator.
5. Repeat for as many folds as you can make.

This type of function is called an exponential function and is of the form $f(x) = a(T)^x$, where

> a = initial amount you start with (the initial thickness)
> T = transformation factor, that is, what happens to the stack of paper (doubles each time)
> x = number of times the change occurs (number of folds)
> $f(x)$ = thickness in inches for x number of folds

The exponential function that depicts this experiment is _____.

Paper Folding (continued)

NAME _____   DATE _____

± ··· ∞ ≈ ∈ ∞ ∅ ± ·· ∞ ≈ ∈ ∞ ∅ ± ·· ∅ ≈ ∈ ∞ ∅ ± ·· ∈ ≈ ∈ ∞ ∅ ± ·· ± ≈ ∈ ∞ ∅ ± ·· ∞ ≈ ∈ ∞ ∅

Use the formula to fill out the table below.

Number of folds	Thickness in inches
0	
1	
2	

Results

How many folds can you actually make?

_____

How does the formula/function allow you to "make more folds"?

_____

Does the thickness of the paper change the number of folds you can make?

_____

What conjecture or conclusion did you come to regarding this experiment?

_____

_____

Algebra Out Loud

Paper Folding (continued)

± ··· ∞ ≈ ∈ ∞ ∅ ± ··· ∞ ≈ ∈ ∞ ∅ ± ··· ∅ ≈ ∈ ∞ ∅ ± ··· ∈ ≈ ∈ ∞ ∅ ± ··· ± ≈ ∈ ∞ ∅ ± ··· ∞ ≈ ∈ ∞ ∅

Use the listing, scatter plot, and regression features of your calculator to do the following activities:

- Sketch the scatter plot and the graph of the function below.

- Predict the thickness of the folded paper for the following number of folds using the table feature of the graph:

Number of Folds	Thickness
10	_____
20	_____
50	_____
100	_____

- Use the table feature of your graphing calculator to approximate the number of folds it would take to obtain a thickness of 1 mile.

_____

- Write up a short report (using at least three complete sentences) explaining the results of your experiment. What have you learned?

Experimenting-to-Learn-Algebra Reports: Building the Perfect Candy Box

NAME _____   DATE _____

ASSIGNMENT: You are to construct open boxes for holding candy.

Requirements

1. Find the dimensions for an open box that will maximize volume.
2. Each box is to be made from precut 2 by 2 feet squares of predecorated cardboard.
3. The box will be made by cutting out a square of side length x in each of the four corners and folding up the edges.

Sketch

Draw a sketch of the problem.

Equation

Find a function for the volume of the box. Call the function $h(x)$:

$h(x) = $ _____

Explanation of the Process

On another sheet of paper, give all steps for maximizing the volume. Explain each step clearly so your boss will understand the process.

Final Report

On another sheet of paper, summarize your findings in a clear report using two to three paragraphs.

Concept Math

WHAT? Description

Concept math is an activity that invites the student to choose a concept and then research and write about the mathematics related to this concept. This activity involves several steps: choosing the concept, researching the concept and the mathematics, freewriting or brainstorming the writing, writing a rough draft, polishing the paper, and sharing the piece with peers and teacher. If the teacher chooses to be a part of each step, the final writing becomes much better. In this case, the concept math paper could be considered a mini research paper.

After students finish writing the paper, they should be encouraged to read the paper out loud to themselves or to a peer. Then after the papers are graded, students might read their papers out loud to the class and demonstrate any mathematics they wrote about in the paper.

WHY? Objectives

The concept math activity allows students the opportunity to:

- Research a concept of their choosing.
- Research and reflect on the mathematics related to their concept.
- Bring personal meaning to algebra.
- Demonstrate creativity regarding algebra and their chosen concept.

HOW? Examples

The topics listed below are ideas of how a student might take a favorite topic and write a paper exploring the mathematics related to that topic. For example, a student might write a paper on a favorite pet (such as bassets) and present the mathematics related to this dog:

Baseball Math	Apple Algebra
Basset Math	Cereal Algebra
Big Foot Math	Pasta Algebra
Guitar Math	Zebra Algebra
Ice Cream Cone Math	Mountain Math
Prayer Math	Sphere Math
Star Math	Valley Girl Math

Concept Math: Basset Math

Basset hounds are short-legged, long-bodied canines of the utmost character. The breed was developed by the French several centuries ago to hunt game in fields or woods with heavy ground cover. Their long ears aid in the hunting of small game as the ears scoop up and their big snouts take in the scent of their prey. Their short barrel-shaped bodies have huge breasts that often rub up against the ground, especially when climbing stairs. Even the basset puppy has huge feet for his or her body. These huge feet are attached to short crooked legs, giving the dog a comical yet adorable appearance.

Female bassets are shorter, weigh less, and tend to have prettier faces than their male counterparts. An adult basset hound weighs between 40 and 100 pounds generally. Bassets tend to live to the ages of twelve to fourteen years.

These dogs are people dogs, very social and loyal. However, they can be stubborn and respond best when offered treats. They see themselves as lap dogs, no matter their size. Their bark turns swiftly into a deep howl when anticipating their master's arrival home or hearing "bad guys" (such as the mail carrier or the garbage collectors). Many bassets' masters register their dogs with the American Kennel Club and name their pets with such titles as King Ralph or Frederick the Great.

Two female bassets named Samantha and Sadie Sue live together. Sam is 14 years old, 57 pounds, is short and chubby, and loves to sleep and eat treats. Sadie Sue is 3 years old, weighs 45 pounds, is taller than Sam and quite lean, and loves to play and terrorize Sam. At least once a day, Sam and Sadie play together, with Sadie doing most of the running and Sam most of the barking. The rest of the time Sadie tries to get Sam's attention, and Sam just tolerates Sadie.

The basset's trunk is cylindrical and usually quite long. The long ears and huge feet are disproportionate to the other dimensions of this dog. Sam's and Sadie Sue's similar shapes are grand examples of the asymetric and cartoonish beauty of the breed, while their personalities are quite typical of this social hound.

Use the basset mathematics from the piece to answer the following questions:

1. Given the small amount of information above, which of the two (Sam or Sadie) is healthier? On a scale of 1 (in bad shape) to 10 (super healthy), rate both dogs' health. Defend your answer.
2. If Sam takes 30 minutes to eat a bone and Sadie Sue takes 15 minutes to eat the same type of bone, how long would it take them to eat the bone if they shared it?
3. Sam and Sadie are tricolored bassets, with white, brown, and black as their configuration. This means they each have mostly white fur and more brown than black fur. How many different tricolor configurations are possible with these three colors? How many four-colored configurations are possible with white, brown, black, and gray?

Learning Logs

WHAT? Description

The creation of a learning log is a writing-to-learn activity that promotes student reflection and analysis of content. A learning log is similar to a journal; however, the emphasis is on content as opposed to students' feelings and opinions of content. Technically, a log is a record of progress or occurrences. In a mathematical learning log, students take notes and answer teacher-generated questions daily, weekly, or periodically. The log is turned in periodically and assigned a grade based mainly on completion rather than accuracy of content.

The learning log may take several different forms: a spiral notebook, a binder of paper, or a file of note cards.

WHY? Objectives

The use of learning logs will allow algebra students to:

- Create a study guide for upcoming assessments.
- Reflect on and summarize key concepts.
- Identify significant concepts and related features and facts from the content.
- Have a dialogue with the teacher regarding content questions or comments.

HOW? Example

Here is an example of a double-entry learning log:

DATE: Sept. 14, 2003

Questions	Answers
Give your definition of a slope.	Slope is the slant of a line. Slope = $\frac{\text{rise}}{\text{run}}$. Slope is difference in 2 y values over difference in 2 x values.
Tell how negative and positive slopes differ.	Positive slope means a line that slants upward. Negative slope means a line that slants downward.

Algebra Out Loud

Writing to Communicate Algebra

$\pm \cdots \infty \approx \in \infty \varnothing \pm \cdots \varnothing \approx \in \infty \varnothing$

6

Prelude

Writing about algebra can be a valuable way for students to think out loud regarding their understanding of algebraic content. Writing to communicate algebra activities allows students to share moments of mathematical clarity or genius with their peers or their instructor. Describing and communicating these thoughts on paper allows them to organize their thoughts and use mathematical vocabulary to enhance and enlarge their mathematical world.

Often we think of communicating mathematically as participating in the aesthetic endeavors of algebra. Poems, short stories, letters, and advertisements regarding algebra are activities that allow the writer to be creative and consider the softer and prettier aspects of algebra.

Writing to communicate algebra is a writing-in-mathematics strategy itself. Student writers must consider the audience and make appropriate choices in mathematical vocabulary and content. When composing a letter to his parents, a student must use more general mathematical terms, unless one parent has a good understanding of the algebra alluded to. Moreover, if a student is composing a poem on the concavity of a graph's curve to be read at a campuswide poetry reading, she might begin by explaining the basic idea of concavity.

This chapter contains the following activities:

Writing across campus

Group exposition

Guided math poetry

Math letters

Math profiling

Math journals

Mathematical investigator

Writing Across Campus

$\pm \cdots \infty \approx \in \infty \emptyset \pm \cdots \infty \approx \in \infty \emptyset \pm \cdots \emptyset \approx \in \infty \emptyset \pm \cdots \in \approx \in \infty \emptyset \pm \cdots \pm \approx \in \infty \emptyset \pm \cdots \infty \approx \in \infty \emptyset$

WHAT? Description

The Writing Across Campus Coffeehouse Readings is an annual activity that takes place at Washburn University in Topeka, Kansas. Each spring semester, several professors and instructors assign an assignment much like this one:

> Create a writing about some concept explored in this class that demonstrates your understanding of the concept. Your piece may be any writing that can be read in a two- to three-minute segment. It may be a poem, rap song, letter, short story, or anything else that can and will be presented at the WU Coffeehouse Readings in April.
>
> If you are interested in reading your piece, please contact the instructor who made this assignment. Or come and listen to and support your peers as they read their creations. Everyone is welcome for an evening of fun, fellowship, and fantastic prose!

Each April, twenty-five to thirty-five students (from the disciplines of science, history, English, social work, and mathematics, to name just a few) come together for coffee, pastries, and poetry and prose readings. From the onset of the Coffeehouse Readings in 1997, mathematics students have volunteered to read their work. Each year, this event is great fun with readings that are funny, sad, enlightening, or even creepy. One year, the majority of readers came from a course called "Bugs and Society." That night the air was full of the imagery of arachnids and creepy crawling things, and everyone left feeling just a little itchy.

WHY? Objectives

Algebra students who write for and read at the Coffeehouse Readings:

- Become better writers and readers.
- Have a chance to consider their chosen concept in a different manner.

- Learn more about their chosen concept and often become experts regarding that concept.

- Learn more about various concepts from different disciplines.

- Are allowed to share personal writings even if they do not consider themselves to be great poets or writers.

- Have a valuable networking experience.

- Experience a unique opportunity to share themselves with each other.

- Share a relaxing evening with their peers and others who are interested in writing and fellowship.

HOW? Examples

The poems that follow were composed for and read at the WU Writing Across the Campus Coffeehouse Readings by three high school students enrolled in a college algebra course.

The Empty Set

Oh, empty set, how lonely you must be,
With nothing between your parenthesy.
Barren and abandoned, dreary and dull,
To bare such a name as null.

When not a number solves the case,
When all other answers are erased,
Without a seven, eight, or nine,
Then it is your time to shine.

You are the answer when there is no solution,
And so I draw the following conclusion:
That you must be important, though you stand alone,
You are well respected and known.

When finding the slope of a vertical line,
No other answer will be mine.
Never to be confused with zero,
Oh, empty set, you are my hero.

Untitled

Finding the domain in college algebra is certainly easy
With two exceptions it's obviously not cheesy
If the problem isn't a fraction or a square root it'll be a snap
Just write down all real numbers and set it on the teacher's lap
Now come the two exceptions to domain
With not too much work domain will definitely be in your reign
The first exception to the rule applies to fractions
The example $y = 1$ over $x + 7$ is a simple attraction
Just make sure that zero isn't on the bottom
When you discover x isn't equal to negative 7, there's the answer to
   your problem
With square root being your final exception to the rule
Simply set the problem as greater than or equal to, now you're no
   fool
Make sure what you're setting it to is either positive or zero
Now you've figured out domain without looking like a weirdo

**raphs**

Graphs are flowers, always growing
Different shapes, various types
Graphs can be a bird soaring,
Ascending and descending
Graphs can be a friendship,
Going through up and down points
They are human life,
Starting low, but ending high.

Graphs are like a radio,
Both can bring bad news
Graphs are much like a telephone,
Both are used to communicate
Graphs are like a stop watch,
Each a great method in recording time
Graphs are like a camera,
Both show actions.

Graphs are like a library,
Both are great tools in teaching and learning
Graphs can be as well done as famous paintings
And as interesting as any mystery
They are as accurate as a road map
And as easy as pie!

Graphs are educational, enlightening,
And absolutely extraordinary!!

Group Exposition

± ··· ∞ ≈ ∈ ∞ ∅ ± ··· ∞ ≈ ∈ ∞ ∅ ± ··· ∅ ≈ ∈ ∞ ∅ ± ··· ∈ ≈ ∈ ∞ ∅ ± ··· ± ≈ ∈ ∞ ∅ ± ··· ∞ ≈ ∈ ∞ ∅

WHAT? Description

A typical algebra course covers from six to twelve chapters and at least fifty different algebraic concepts. Often, there is very little time to include historical anecdotes or real-world applications of the concepts presented. One solution to this dilemma is to require small groups of students to research and write up this material and then present it to their peers.

The group exposition activity works best with groups of two or three students with clearly defined roles. The roles might include researcher, writer, and editor-reporter. The assigned roles ensure that everyone in the group contributes to the exposition. Small amounts of class time should be allocated for groups to choose roles, brainstorm, assign tasks, and share work that has been completed outside class. Students may choose the format for the presentation: essay or speech, poster presentation, and skit or play are a few ideas. Students can build on the talents of the group members and choose a format that is compatible with those talents.

Let's say that the exposition topic is the history of the number pi. The researcher gathers, reads, and takes notes from resources related to this history. The writer takes this material and composes the essay, poster presentation, or play. Finally, the editor-reporter edits the writer's work and presents the finished exposition to the class.

In a class of twenty-four students, eight expositions could be assigned over the semester. Approximately every other week, a different group could present an exposition on a concept being taught during that period. Students could use allocated class time or a time when other students are doing seat work to prepare. Multiple resources should be made available to students for this preparation.

WHY? Objectives

The group exposition activity allows the algebra student to:

- Learn from and teach to peers.

- Research and reshape relevant material.

- Learn more about the history and applications of the concepts in the course.

- Collaborate with peers and develop good group work skills.

The group exposition activity allows the mathematics teacher to:

- Share a more holistic picture of the concept with students.
- Teach and encourage valuable group skills.
- Learn from students' expositions.
- Assess the students' understanding of the concept.

HOW? Examples

Here are some possible topics for this activity:

- History of Pi
- Applications of Imaginary Numbers in Today's World
- History of Algebra
- Historical Applications of Linear Programming
- History of Prime Numbers
- Applications of the Quadratic Formula in Today's World
- History of the Pythagorean Theorem

Group Exposition

NAME _____   DATE _____

± ·· ∞ ≈ ∈ ∞ ∅ ± ·· ∞ ≈ ∈ ∞ ∅ ± ·· ∅ ≈ ∈ ∞ ∅ ± ·· ∈ ≈ ∈ ∞ ∅ ± ·· ± ≈ ∈ ∞ ∅ ± ·· ∞ ≈ ∈ ∞ ∅

ASSIGNMENT: Each group will be given one chapter to choose a topic from for a presentation to the class. The topic might be the history of one of the algebraic concepts or an application that uses the algebra introduced in this chapter.

Your group must choose the format for the presentation: essay or speech, poster presentation, or skit or play, for example. Your presentation will take place sometime during the time that we cover that particular chapter. When you have selected a topic and format, please see me.

Also, you are to assign the following roles in your group: researcher, writer, and editor-reporter. Some class time will be allocated for work on this project; see the class calendar for these dates.

Listed below are the chapters to be covered in the text and some suggested topics:

Chapter	Chapter Title	Suggested Topics
1	From Data to Equations	History of linear equations History of correlation and the line of best fit Application of correlation
2	Operations with Numbers and Functions	History of functions History of exponents Application of a function
3	Equations and Functions	History of inverse function History of composition function History of symmetry and mathematics Application of symmetry
4	Matrices and Systems of Equations	History of matrices History of systems of equations History of linear programming Application of matrix algebra
5	Quadratic Functions	History of the quadratic function History of the imaginary number History of the quadratic formula Application of the quadratic function
6	Polynomial Functions	History of the polynomial function History of graphing polynomials Application of the polynomial function
7	Exponential and Logarithmic Functions	History of exponential functions History of logarithms Application of logarithms
8	Trigonometric Functions	History of trigonometry History of radian measure Application of right triangle trigonometry

Chapters from *Advanced Algebra* by Ellis, Schultz, and Hollowell.

Guided Math Poetry

WHAT? Description

The creation and sharing of mathematical poetry can be an extraordinary learning experience for teacher and students. This writing activity has the teacher guide the student writer through the process of creating a mathematical poem. Writing math poetry can provide students with a forum for expressing themselves, as well as considering the vocabulary related to a mathematical concept. It can prove to be a pleasant respite from the daily routine. By reading or listening to students' poetry, teachers are able to pinpoint student misconceptions about the chosen concepts and experience the mathematics through the words of the student poets.

WHY? Objectives

The creation of math poetry allows the mathematics student to:

- Express concepts in his or her own words.
- Consider the unique qualities or features of a math concept.
- See mathematics in a new light.
- Merge his or her creative talents with mathematical skills.
- Become a communicator of mathematics.

Reading or hearing students' math poetry allows the teacher to:

- See mathematical concepts through the eyes of students.
- Pinpoint and correct student misconceptions.
- Appreciate the diverse skills or talents of students.
- Promote communication in mathematics and foster good communication skills.

HOW? Examples

The two lessons that follow give the prompts used to guide students through the creation of math poetry.

Guided Math Poetry: Creating Math Cinquains

± ··· ∞ ≈ ∈ ∞ ∅ ± ··· ∞ ≈ ∈ ∞ ∅ ± ··· ∅ ≈ ∈ ∞ ∅ ± ··· ∈ ≈ ∈ ∞ ∅ ± ··· ± ≈ ∈ ∞ ∅ ± ··· ∞ ≈ ∈ ∞ ∅

A cinquain is a five-line stanza or portion of a poem. (This activity is adapted from Mac-Beth, Harris, Helmlich, and Newsome, 1997.)

Teacher Directions	**Example**
"Write down a math noun. Recall that a noun is the name of a person, place, or thing."	exponent
"Write out two words that describe your noun."	positive, negative
"Now write three verbs that go with your noun. Recall that verbs are action words."	squared, cubed, powered
"Now write a phrase that says something about your original noun."	raises to some real or imaginary number
"Finally, rewrite your noun or a synonym of your noun."	exponent

"Now, put it all together and you have created a poem!"

> Exponent
> Positive, negative
> Squared, cubed, powered
> Raises to some real or imaginary number
> Exponent

Here are some examples of algebraic cinquains:

> algebra
> abstract, generalized
> functions, multiplies, squares
> the mathematics of symbols and problem solving
> algebra

Creating Math Cinquains (continued)

NAME _____   DATE _____

graph
linear, parabolic
planed, coordinated, plotted
a model of life as points on a plane
graph

matrix
augmented, inverse
solving, inverting, transforming
a rectangular array that represents a system
matrix

number
singular, plural
tallying, summing, adding
for counting my things, my worldly worth
one

empty set
vacuous, illusive
hides, plunders, assassinates
a black hole of confusion and mind pirates
no solution

Guided Math Poetry: Math Wordplay

NAME _____ DATE _____

±···∞≈∈∞∅±···∞≈∈∞∅±···∅≈∈∞∅±···∈≈∈∞∅±···±≈∈∞∅±···∞≈∈∞∅

Wordplay is a writing activity borrowed and adapted from Amy Fleury's creative writing course at Washburn University (2000).

Teacher Directions	Example
"Write down three math nouns. Recall that nouns are subjects or things."	number, product, solution
"Change each noun to a verb by adding a suffix. Made-up words are allowed."	numbered, producting, solutioned
"Now use at least two of your words in phrases."	Secretly, she solutioned his demise. His days would soon be numbered.
"Write down three math verbs. Recall that verbs are action words."	add, solve, prove
"Change each verb to a noun by adding prefixes or suffixes."	adding, solvation, proveness
"Now, use two of these 'nouns' in phrases that might fit with your last phrases."	A chemical crime with no solvation. The proveness would allude all others.
"Write down three math adjectives. Recall that adjectives are words that describe."	finite, positive, negative
"Change each adjective to either a noun or a verb."	finitation, positiving, negativing
"Now, use two of these in phrases."	She reveled in his nearing finitation. Only then would she be positiving her life!

"Finally, use some or all of your phrases to put together a prose poem."

> Secretly, she solutioned his demise
> His days would soon be numbered
> A chemical crime with no solvation
> The proveness would allude all others.
> She reveled in his nearing finitation
> Only then would she be positiving her life!

Math Letters

WHAT? Description

One of the more obvious vehicles for communication is the written letter. Asking students to write letters about particular topics in mathematics is asking them to communicate what they have learned. Student letter writers must research and reflect on content, summarize their understanding of the topic, and compose a writing that is readable and understandable to the reader.

Math letters may be composed for real or imaginary recipients. When students actually compose and send their letters to friends or family, they take great care in choosing the words to clearly explain their topic. They then must consider the knowledge or lack of knowledge of mathematics of their audience. Often high school and college algebra students know more mathematics than their parents ever will.

The assignment should be explicit in terms of audience, theme, and format (with guidelines on length, typed or longhand, formal or informal writing style, and so forth). If possible, share an example of an A letter with students after giving the assignment.

WHY? Objectives

The writing of a letter about mathematics allows the mathematics student to:

- Research and reflect on a particular mathematical topic.
- Practice communicating mathematics.
- Summarize knowledge of a particular mathematical topic.
- Carefully consider the audience while composing the letter.

The reading of a math letter composed by a student allows the teacher to:

- Assess the student's understanding of the math topic.
- Pinpoint the student's misconceptions of the math topic.
- Comment in writing regarding the student's understanding or misunderstanding of the math topic.
- Engage in a dialogue with a student who may be hesitant to ask questions of the instructor face to face or in front of peers.

HOW? Examples

Let us say that the assignment is to compose an informal letter, one page in length. The letter must be typed double-spaced and contain at least three paragraphs. It should be clear and use vocabulary based on the knowledge of the audience.

Here are some examples of assignments to various audiences:

- Write a letter to an absent student explaining the process of finding the inverse of a function.
- Write a letter to a prospective employer detailing your knowledge of linear programming and how that knowledge will help her company. Use a formal tone.
- Write a letter to your parents explaining how a graphing calculator will help you learn algebra. Your goal is to convince them to buy you one.
- Write a letter to your teacher comparing and contrasting logarithmic and exponential functions.
- Write a letter to the president explaining how algebra could help him win the next election.
- Write a letter to your last math teacher detailing what you have learned about graphing in college algebra.

Math Letters: Memo to Your Boss

NAME _____   DATE _____

± ⋯ ∞ ≈ ∈ ∞ ∅ ± ⋯ ∞ ≈ ∈ ∞ ∅ ± ⋯ ∅ ≈ ∈ ∞ ∅ ± ⋯ ∈ ≈ ∈ ∞ ∅ ± ⋯ ± ≈ ∈ ∞ ∅ ± ⋯ ∞ ≈ ∈ ∞ ∅

ASSIGNMENT: Your boss, the president of Beowulf Basset Chow, sends this memo to you:

MEMORANDUM

FROM: Office of the President of Beowulf Basset Chow

TO: Employee X

Develop a method or formula(s) for the cost and profit of manufacturing cans of our new dog food: Basset Beefcakes. We want each case to sell for $15. It takes $7 for the food and packaging material of each case, and the shipping cost for up to 200 cases is a flat $400. How many cases must we sell to start making a profit? We need this information ASAP!

Compose a memo in response. This is your opportunity to become known as something other than Employee X to the president. Assume his mathematical knowledge is limited. However, be clear, not condescending!

Here is a hint: Write two linear equations in two variables and graph.

MEMORANDUM

FROM: Employee X

TO: Office of the President of Beowulf Basset Chow

Math Letters

$\pm \cdots \infty \approx \in \infty \varnothing \pm \cdots \infty \approx \in \infty \varnothing \pm \cdots \varnothing \approx \in \infty \varnothing \pm \cdots \in \approx \in \infty \varnothing \pm \cdots \pm \approx \in \infty \varnothing \pm \cdots \infty \approx \in \infty \varnothing$

ASSIGNMENT: Write a letter to your parents explaining why college algebra is an important class for you regarding your future courses and career(s.) Use at least five of the following algebra topics in your letter. Your letter should be at least one page or four paragraphs in length. Consider the mathematical knowledge of your parents as you choose words to describe or explain these topics. The letter must be typed and in a proper letter format. Use an English text to remind you of this format.

ALGEBRA TOPICS

graph
real numbers
integers
equation
linear equation
quadratic equation
exponent
inverse
matrix
linear programming
logarithm
sequence
series

GRADING: The final draft of the letter is worth _____ points.
DUE DATES: The rough draft is due on _____.
The final draft is due on _____.

Math Profiling

WHAT? Description

A profile is a short biographical character sketch or piece of writing detailing the relevant data concerning a particular person, place, or thing. Writing profiles are usually about persons, places, or activities in the community. They may focus on a person in the community who uses mathematics at work, a place where mathematics is employed in its daily operations, or an activity where mathematics is a vital component of the event. Just as criminal profiling is used as a method for uncovering the characteristics and, perhaps, the identity of a criminal, math profiling can be used to uncover the mathematics used in a particular career or activity and help students make educated choices in their future careers.

A math profile should contain the following information:

- The name of the person, place, or event and descriptive information
- The rationale for profiling this person, place, or event
- The mathematics associated with this subject
- Any interesting anecdotes regarding the subject
- Any accomplishments or honors associated with the subject

The creation of a math profile involves several steps:

1. Find a topic for the profile, using the library, the Internet, directories, persons, or resources in the community.
2. Make a plan of action by setting goals and establishing a time line.
3. Write out questions for interviewing persons or researching activities.
4. Interview or collect information on the subject of interest.
5. Take notes.
6. Organize information, prepare an outline, and compose a rough draft.

7. Revise, edit, peer review, and proofread the profile.

8. Read the profile out loud to yourself, and polish the final draft.

WHY? Objectives

Creating a math profile requires that the algebra student:

- Research, write, and learn about a particular person, place, or event in the community.
- Practice establishing and carrying out a plan, setting goals, and meeting deadlines.
- Prewrite, write, and rewrite a mathematical profile.
- Learn about mathematics in the community and possible career options or opportunities.

HOW? Examples

Here are examples of persons, places, or activities for math profiles.

Person	Place	Activity
Chemist at RX, Inc.	RX, Inc.	Trials for new cancer drug
Dr. Math, math professor	Mathematics Department at Smalltown University	Math Day, local math contest for area high school math students
Ms. Eureka, president of the State Association of Teachers of Mathematics (SATM)	SATM central office	Annual State Mathematics Conference
Mr. Dollar, county treasurer	County Treasury Department	April 15 any year

Math Profiling

± ·· ∞ ≈ ∈ ∞ ∅ ± ·· ∞ ≈ ∈ ∞ ∅ ± ·· ∅ ≈ ∈ ∞ ∅ ± ·· ∈ ≈ ∈ ∞ ∅ ± ·· ± ≈ ∈ ∞ ∅ ± ·· ∞ ≈ ∈ ∞ ∅

ASSIGNMENT: Use the worksheet shown here to help compose your math profile. Be sure to fill in each blank.

Profile topic (person, place, or activity)
Plan of action   (brief description of your plan for researching and composing profile)
Deadlines   Interview or observation day = _____   Rough draft due = _____   Peer review date = _____   Final draft due = _____
Interview or on-site questions
Research notes
Peer review comments *(see attached peer review form)*
Final analysis or self-evaluation of profile

Math Profiling

NAME _____   DATE _____

$\pm \cdots \infty \approx \in \infty \varnothing \pm \cdots \infty \approx \in \infty \varnothing \pm \cdots \varnothing \approx \in \infty \varnothing \pm \cdots \in \approx \in \infty \varnothing \pm \cdots \pm \approx \in \infty \varnothing \pm \cdots \infty \approx \in \infty \varnothing$

ASSIGNMENT: Find a mathematician; a city or country of a great mathematical invention; or a mathematical invention, discovery, or activity from the past for your math profile. Use the worksheet shown here to help compose your math profile. Be sure to fill in each blank.

Profile topic (person, place, or activity)

Plan of action
(brief description of your plan for researching and composing profile)

Deadlines
Interview or observation day = _____
Rough draft due = _____
Peer review date = _____
Final draft due = _____

Questions (answers will come from your research)

Research notes

Peer review comments *(see attached peer review form)*

Final analysis or self-evaluation of profile

Math Profiling: Peer Review Sheet

NAME _____   DATE _____

Peer reviewing is used to help the profiler-writer self-assess the profile. Fill in the table shown here, keeping in mind that your comments will assist the profiler.

Questions	Yes/No
Paper is well organized and neat.	
Subject is a good choice for a math profile.	
Paper is well written, with few grammar and spelling errors.	
Paper contains all required components.	
Paper contains the appropriate mathematical connections.	
Paper is interesting.	

What I liked best about your profile was

_____

_____

One thing I would change is

_____

_____

Math Journals

WHAT? Description

A journal is a periodic record in which the writer documents experiences and chronicles her or his thoughts, feelings, and opinions regarding these activities. Entries in the journal are written on a daily, weekly, or monthly basis. The math journal is usually a weekly log that allows a forum for dialogue between student and teacher. The content to be recorded in a math journal differs from instructor to instructor. Some journal assignments ask for student reflection, some call for comments regarding content, and others ask for a combination of the two.

The reflective math journal gives students a forum for expressing positive and negative reactions to learning. Each week, the assignment might be the same: students are to express their thoughts or feelings about the teaching and learning of algebra for that week only. Or the teacher may elect to use prompts to help direct the student writers to focus on one or more particular aspect—for example:

- How do you feel about taking this algebra course?
- Describe yourself as a learner of mathematics.
- Evaluate your progress so far in this course.
- What problems did you encounter in class this week?
- Write about your mathematical strengths and weaknesses in algebra.
- Describe the effort you put into this algebra course this semester. Then rate your effort on a scale from 0 to 10, where 0 = no effort, 5 = average effort, and 10 = 100% effort.

A journal assignment that requires the writer to demonstrate understanding of algebraic content allows the teacher to observe and respond to students' misconceptions or use of unique methods for problem solving. Here are several examples of prompts for students to refer to algebraic content:

- Compare and contrast the slope of a horizontal and a vertical line. Write out your answer in at least two complete paragraphs. Then give an example of an equation and graph for each.

- Write out in words the method for solving the following equation: $ax + b = 0$, where a and b are positive real numbers. Then give an explanation of why it is important to know that a and b are positive.
- Discuss the concavity of the graph of the following function: $y = 2x^2 - 8$. Use words and sketches, and be clear!
- Describe the process for finding the maximum or minimum value of a polynomial function using a graphing calculator. Use whichever calculator (for example, TI 83) you usually use in this class. Give all steps.

Here are some examples of prompts for combination journals:

- Writing mathematics is considerably more difficult than ordinary writing. Do you agree? Defend your opinion.
- Write out your general process for solving a word problem. Then, choose a problem from pages 215–217, solve the problem, and write out all the steps of your problem-solving process. Please write as if you were explaining the process to a student who was absent the day we reviewed this material in class.

All writing requirements for journal entries, such as length of response or use of complete sentences, should be given at the outset of the course or the journal assignment.

All teachers, whether they are novices or seasoned in this activity, will benefit from the following hints when assigning a math journal:

- Plan your time well. The reading of and responding to thirty journal entries each week takes time.
- Choose only one course each semester to incorporate the math journal into the curriculum.
- If you ask students to comment on the course or the teaching, be prepared to read unflattering comments.
- Collect journals on Friday (or the end of the week) and return on Monday (or the beginning of the week.) When you are consistent, students understand that you believe in the importance of this assignment.
- Have all students use the same type of book for the journal, such as a spiral notebook or a blue book. Avoid having students use papers placed in looseleaf binders because they tend to lose entries or mix class notes in with journal entries.

- Use a box with handles or tote with which to collect and carry the journals.
- Give credit or points for journal entries. Often students will consider ungraded assignments as busywork and will respond in kind.
- Use journals only if you are a true believer—that is, you believe that writing is a powerful teaching and learning tool in mathematics.

WHY? Objectives

Math journals allow the student writer:

- To express negative and positive feelings about the course.
- A forum for dialogue with the teacher.
- To self-assess his or her progress in the course.
- A forum for writing to learn algebra.

Math journals allow the teacher:

- To authentically assess student comprehension and progress.
- To hear and address student dissatisfaction in the course.
- A forum for dialogue with each student.
- To catch individual student errors early and in a nonthreatening manner.

HOW? Examples

The lessons that follow give examples of assignments and student journal entries.

Math Journals

NAME _____   DATE _____

ASSIGNMENT: Over the semester, you are to keep a mathematics journal. Each week, write a one- to two-page journal entry in a spiral notebook.

OBJECTIVE: The math journal will allow you a forum for having a dialogue with me over the semester. Please use the journal to ask questions of or give comments to me as needed.

DUE DATES: On Wednesday, a journal prompt, in the form of a question(s), will be given. You are to write your response and hand in your notebook with each weekly entry in it on Friday. On the following Monday, all journals will be handed back. Due dates will be announced on shortened weeks or weeks containing holidays.

GRADING: Each entry is worth 5 points according to the following criteria:

Mechanics (grammar, spelling, transitions)	2 points
Accuracy (regarding content or use of math terms)	2 points
Follows guidelines (see rules below)	1 point
Total	5 points

Fifteen entries will be assigned over the semester. The math journal constitutes approximately one-eighth or 12.5% of the course grade.

JOURNAL ENTRY GUIDELINES: Each entry:

- Must be at least three-quarters of a page and at most two pages in length.

- Must contain complete sentences and at least two paragraphs.

- Must answer each question or prompt completely. Often there will be two prompts. Answer both!

- Should contain as many math terms as possible.

- May include graphs, sketches, and algebraic work in response to the question.

- Must be legible. Please print if your writing is hard to read.

Math Journals (continued)

$\pm \cdots \infty \approx \in \infty \varnothing \pm \cdots \infty \approx \in \infty \varnothing \pm \cdots \varnothing \approx \in \infty \varnothing \pm \cdots \in \approx \in \infty \varnothing \pm \cdots \pm \approx \in \infty \varnothing \pm \cdots \infty \approx \in \infty \varnothing$

FIRST ENTRY PROMPT

1. Think back to your first experiences learning arithmetic in elementary school. Write out a description of yourself as an early learner of mathematics. Then describe yourself as a learner of mathematics today.

2. Which set of numbers, the real numbers or the integers, is larger? Defend your answer.

Math Journals

NAME _____   DATE _____

$\pm \cdots \infty \approx \in \infty \emptyset \pm \cdots \infty \approx \in \infty \emptyset \pm \cdots \emptyset \approx \in \infty \emptyset \pm \cdots \in \approx \in \infty \emptyset \pm \cdots \pm \approx \in \infty \emptyset \pm \cdots \infty \approx \in \infty \emptyset$

ASSIGNMENT: Each student is to keep a math journal in the blue examination books handed out the first day of class. The journal will consist of weekly entries, each one to two pages in length. All writing must be in complete sentences and contain as many math terms as possible. Each entry will contain responses to one or more of the following questions:

- Summarize the mathematics studied during the past week in two or three paragraphs.

- Work out one problem from the homework assignment. Choose one that you need help on if possible.

- Give the reaction to the algebra studied this past week. Was it easy to understand? What was the hardest part of the week's lesson? How would you rate your progress and understanding? Write out any questions you have regarding this material.

DUE DATES:

The journal questions will be given on Friday.

Each entry (in the journal) is to be handed in on Monday.

Journals will be handed back on Wednesday.

GRADING:

Each entry is worth 3 points. The journal grade will comprise 20% of the course grade.

COMMENTS:

The ability to communicate effectively is probably one of the most valuable skills you possess. The math journal gives you a forum for honing this skill.

Self-assessment is another valuable skill. Each entry calls for some form of self-assessment.

Please consider the journal your opportunity to ask questions that you were unable to ask during class.

Math Journals: Assignment

NAME _____ DATE _____

WHAT? The journal will be reflective with weekly written reactions to readings from the book *A Beautiful Mind* (Nasar, 1998).

HOW? Each entry must be at least two paragraphs in length and contain complete and clear sentences with good transitions.

WHY? This excellent novel describes the life story of a gifted yet mentally ill mathematician. It also gives a superb overview of the mathematics of the twentieth century and insight into many gifted mathematicians' thinking. Look for and comment on these inferences when possible.

WHEN? Each entry is due on Monday and will be handed back on the next class day.

HOW MUCH? The journal is worth 50 points, or 10% of the course grade.

Students were asked to write about their understanding of functions. The following quotations are excerpts from these entries (Mower, 1996):

- Some entries demonstrated students' conjectures:

    "I was unaware of the numerous types of functions. . . . I wrote each down individually and was surprised at the number of types of problems which fall under the label of a function. Up until now I was doing the problems . . . wondering what the whole picture was in the building process. Now I am enlightened . . . of the correlation between all functions."

    "$y = x$ is a line and $y = x^2$ is a parabola . . . $y = x^{n>2}$ must have the shape of a wave!"

- Students used the journal to pose questions:

    "I understood the examples of years in college increase your salary, or weight varies with age . . . could this be a function: Your interest in functions increases your understanding?"

    "I was a little confused about the horizontal asymptote . . . it would cover the whole line . . . from right to left, without any holes. . . . So, a line could cross the H.A., but would it be a point . . . or an open circle?"

- Some journal entries displayed students' moments of genius or at least of creativity. The following entries give definitions of a circle:

    "A neverending line that curves perfectly to meet at the start and continues in the same pattern."

    "A circle is a perfection, no end and no beginning. The shape of the largest objects in the universe. The sun, the stars. A perfect curve. A two-dimensional view of a sphere."

- The following excerpts come from journal entries regarding writing in mathematics in a writing-intensive algebra course:

    "I liked this more than any of my other math courses because we learned more . . . we wrote things down and we did things differently and it helped me to remember things."

    "When you write things down it is like encoding. A person is more likely to remember when they write it . . . the steps and rules from our lectures."

- Some students used the journal to write about their emotion regarding the learning of algebra:

    "Today was the first day of new material and I feel overwhelmed."

    "Last week was like a rollercoaster for me as far as understanding. During your lecture, I felt as if I had a decent idea of concepts and methods . . . my problem is that once I leave class I forget."

Mathematical Investigator

WHAT? Description

Investigative writing begins with questioning and data collection, and ends with a written report presenting this knowledge. During the investigation period, others' opinions or reactions are amassed; however, the writer usually abstains from giving his or her thoughts on the subject of investigation. "Just the facts, ma'am!" Overall, the purpose of investigating is to discover facts, and the purpose of investigative writing is to present these facts. The very phrase *investigative reporting* brings to mind tabloid news or, at the very least, the uncovering of secrets. The study of algebra may seem to hold secrets to some. Certainly, the number of people on earth who understand mathematics at a level higher than college algebra is relatively small, which is a wonderful fact to share with your algebra students!

Investigative writing includes some or all of the following techniques:

- Choose a subject: a person, place, concept, or process having to do with algebra—for example, the Arabic contribution to the field of algebra or the concept of the slope of a line.

- Ask and answer the "wh" questions, such as *what, where, when,* and *why.*

- Summarize or take notes from sources and record sources in the appropriate format.

- Use a title and an introduction that grab the attention of the reader.

- State the main theme, hypothesis, or purpose of the investigation.

- Analyze (break it up into its parts), synthesize (put the parts back into a whole of your understanding), and summarize the unearthed facts and data regarding the algebraic topic.

- Consider the audience, and write the report using vocabulary that is easily understood by this audience. Read your report out loud so as to catch and correct grammatical errors.

Remember that an investigative report is a news story detailing the known or, at times, surmised information regarding a topic in algebra. The report does not need to be a written report; it may take the simpler form of an ad or a song or the more formal research paper. An assignment sheet should be given to each student writer detailing the writing expectations or grading criteria.

Note that the proof by scientific investigation process (in geometry and algebra) is very similar to the reporting process described above. Proof by scientific investigation includes the following steps, with the corresponding components of the process above given in parentheses:

1. Investigating and observation (researching)
2. Conjecturing (formulating hypotheses)
3. Testing and belief (testing and choosing hypotheses)
4. Informal explanation (composing outline or rough draft)
5. Proof (completing final write-up)

WHY? Objectives

The mathematical investigation activity allows the algebra student:

- Another format for the demonstration of algebraic understanding.
- An opportunity to consider or see algebra in a new form.
- A forum for expressing and demonstrating interest in algebraic concepts.
- An opportunity to learn how to compose an investigative report.

HOW? Examples

The lessons that follow have suggested topics and an assignment sheet.

Mathematical Investigator

Algebraic Topics	**Tabloid Headlines** (In other words, don't take this assignment so seriously!!!!!!)
Empty set	"The Empty Set Unveiled!"
Prime number	"True Prime: A Career in Crime"
Slope	"He Slipped on the Slippery Slope of Life"
Domain	"She Entered into His Domain, Never to Be Seen Again"
Prime	"Exposed as Prime Suspect in Numbers Racket"
Power	"Extrema Power"
Square	"Cult Found Squaring the Circle"
Symmetry	"Twins Cloned Symmetry Revealed!"

Possible hypotheses and/or thesis statements:

- The empty set was created by a mathematician who had trouble solving math problems.
- There is an infinite amount of primes, and the calculator cannot give a "last" one.
- "Any number raised to zero power is equal to 1" was invented by a person, not discovered.
- Most models do not have faces with "real" reflection symmetry.

Mathematical Investigator

NAME _____   DATE _____

ASSIGNMENT: Choose an algebraic concept for the topic of a mathematical/scientific investigative report. Complete the matrix below, and use this information to write a 3- to 4-paragraph report in response to your thesis statement. Be sure to write an introduction and a conclusion. Consider your audience to be the students in this class.

Subject	
What, when, where	
Why	
Hypothesis	
Investigative notes	
Thesis statement	

Algebra Out Loud

± ··· ∞ ≈ ∈ ∞ ∅ ± ··· ∅ ≈ ∈ ∞ ∅ **7**

Writing as
Authentic Assessment

Prelude

To assess student work is to assign value or credit to this work based on some sort of continuum, usually numerical. This assessment value is usually documented and reported to the student and other interested parties. This measurement is used for determination of student's immediate or future placement and/or graduation. However, to authentically assess is to assign qualitative worth to individual or group effort and work.

Authentic means genuine or real. Authentic assessment of an individual student involves the painting of a portrait that reveals the student's learning goals, habits, skills, and interests, that is, a picture of the real learner. Through the authentic assessment of individual students, teachers are able to pinpoint and address learning weaknesses and build on learning strengths. Moreover, through authentic assessment of larger groups of students, teachers are better able to plan effective approaches and time lines for the teaching and learning of algebra or certain algebraic concepts.

Students who learn to authentically assess themselves as learners also become better able to build on their strengths and address their weaknesses in learning. Authentic assessment of oneself is called *metacognition*. Students who reflect on themselves as learners of mathematics build metacognitive skills and become more productive learners.

The writing activities in this chapter address three types of authentic assessment (some of the activities will be of more than one of these types):

- Teacher's assessment of the progress of the algebra class as a whole and, thus, a self-assessment as a teacher of algebra
- Teacher's assessment of an individual algebra student's learning progress
- Student's assessment of self as a learner of algebra and progress in the course

This chapter contains the following activities:

Muddiest point

Math analogies

One-minute summary

Math is a four-letter word

E-writing

Math similes, metaphors, and analogies

Targeted problem-solving assessments

Self-portrait as a learner of algebra

Muddiest Point

WHAT? Description

The Muddiest Point (Angelo and Cross, 1993) is an activity that allows the teacher to assess student comprehension of the content addressed in a classroom discussion or lesson. Students are given a 3- by 5-inch index card at the end of a day's lesson and asked to write out the most confusing topic from that lesson. Students hand in the cards as they leave the classroom. The teacher reads the cards sometime before preparing the next day's lesson. Often, the cards reveal one or two topics that several students found unclear. This point or points of confusion may be addressed in the next lesson or, if time permits, a review of these topics may become the next lesson.

WHY? Objectives

The Muddiest Point activity allows the teacher to:

- Authentically assess student comprehension of content.
- Address common problems and adapt the next lesson accordingly.
- Address weaknesses or confusion in future instruction.

The Muddiest Point activity allows the mathematics student to:

- Review notes and pinpoint unclear material from the lesson.
- Share points of confusion with the instructor.
- Have an opportunity to hear confusing content in another manner.

HOW? Examples

In answer to the prompt "For me the most difficult topic in this unit [on solving simple linear equations] is . . . ," students wrote, for example:

Word problems, word problems, word problems!!
Circles

Circles finding area and radius

Application problems

Functions

Graphing calculator and functions

And in answer to the prompt "For me the easiest topic in this unit is . . . ," they wrote:

Functions

Linear functions

Graphing functions

Domain and range

Muddiest Point

±···∞≈∈∞∅±···∞≈∈∞∅±··∅≈∈∞∅±·∈≈∈∞∅±···±≈∈∞∅±···∞≈∈∞∅

The muddiest point presented in class today was:

The easiest thing presented in class today was:

Math Analogies

WHAT? Description

Having students create math analogies is an enjoyable as well as instructional activity that may be used to relieve anxiety. An analogy demonstrates a similarity between things that are normally considered dissimilar.

On the first day of a mathematics course, students might be asked to complete a statement like this: "Doing math is like . . ." Some responses might be

". . . swimming upstream,"
". . . skipping on the beach," or
". . . eating chocolate"

Having students share these responses with their peers is a novel way to start a course that some students might consider to be boring or difficult. Usually the sharing of analogies sparks a lively discussion. The exploration of analogies can also reinforce student comprehension of mathematical terms.

Students need to know the definition of terms before they are able to consider appropriate metaphors or analogies.

WHY? Objectives

Creating math analogies gives the algebra student an opportunity to:

- Start the course in a pleasant and nonthreatening manner.
- Consider mathematical concepts in a different manner.
- Think deeply regarding the definitions of concepts.
- Hear and consider peers' analogies.
- Identify and practice metacognitive skills.

HOW? Examples

Some examples are good for getting students started:

Earning an A in this course would be like _____.

Solving a mathematical problem is like _____.

Factoring a quadratic is like _____.

A function is to a graph like a _____ is to a _____.

A parabola is to a quadratic function like a _____ is to a _____.

A solution is to an equation like a _____ is to a _____.

A function is to a relation as a _____ is to a _____.

Math Analogies: Linear Equations

NAME _____   DATE _____

ASSIGNMENT: Fill in the blanks using the words below. In some cases, more than one word or expression will work. However, write only one word or expression for each blank.

Words and Expressions

square	orange	color
area	lemon	apple
slant	cat	size
line segment	kitten	Fido
$ax + by = c$	wedge	Sadie Sue
ramp	ladder	garage
$y = mx + b$	house	paint brush
$(y - y^1) = m(x - x^1)$	paw	roller
side	basset hound	number
circle	dog	zero
radius	zero slope	boy
ground	flat	woman

A line is to a point as a _____ is to a _____.

The length of a line segment is like the _____ of a _____.

A slope is to a line as a _____ is to a _____.

The point slope form is to the slope intercept form as _____ is to

_____.

Parallel is to perpendicular as _____ is to _____.

Parallel lines are to equal slopes as perpendicular lines are to _____ slopes.

x intercept is to a line as _____ is to a _____.

x intercept is to y intercept as _____ is to _____.

A linear function is to vertical line as _____ is to _____.

A horizontal line is to slope as a _____ is to _____.

One-Minute Summary

$\pm\cdots\infty\approx\in\infty\emptyset\pm\cdots\infty\approx\in\infty\emptyset\pm\cdots\emptyset\approx\in\infty\emptyset\pm\cdots\in\approx\in\infty\emptyset\pm\cdots\pm\approx\in\infty\emptyset\pm\cdots\infty\approx\in\infty\emptyset$

WHAT? Description

The one-minute summary is a familiar assignment for English and writing teachers. Often called the one-minute essay, this brief writing exercise yields a wealth of student knowledge to the writer and the reader. The teacher asks the student to free-write (write without worrying about grammar or spelling errors) on a particular topic. One-minute summaries may be assigned at the beginning, middle, or end of a classroom lecture or demonstration. Often, a teacher will assign this writing at the beginning and at the end of a lesson. The student writer is then able to self-assess his or her progress in learning the lesson. One-minute summaries are handed in for the teacher to scan but usually are not graded.

WHY? Objectives

One-minute summaries allow mathematics students to:

- Free-associate and free-write about a particular math topic.
- Self-assess their comprehension of a concept or lesson.
- Write without worrying about grammar or spelling.
- Write without worrying about a grade.
- Demonstrate their comprehension of a topic to the teacher.

One-minute summaries allow the teacher to:

- Authentically assess each student's understanding of a concept.
- Pinpoint misconceptions of a concept.
- Respond to individual students or the class regarding common misconceptions.
- Reassess and reshape future lessons on this topic.

HOW? Examples

The teacher might begin this activity, "Take out a clean sheet of paper. We are going to free-write for exactly one minute on one topic. To free-write means to write continuously without worrying about grammar rules or correct spellings. Just write everything you think or know about the following topic, without stopping your pencil."

Here are some sample topics:

slope

quadratics equation

parabola

synthetic division

imaginary unit

empty set

matrix

One-Minute Summary: Student Summaries of Rational Numbers

Student Summaries

"Rational numbers are anything that can be put into a fraction."

"All numbers that can be expressed as a fraction and that can be divided by itself."

"A rational number is any number that can be expressed as a fraction. It can be 1, –2, 3 or 4. I don't think 0 is a rational number because you can't say 0 over 2!"

"Rational #'s are any numbers that can be written in the form of a/b, a & b being Integers are R as they can be over 1."

Teacher Comments

"Rational #'s can also be integers."

"Actually all numbers can be divided by themselves. We want a fraction of integers."

"Yes, you can write 0/2 which is equal to 0. So, 0 is a rational number. You may be confusing 0/2 with 2/0 which is impossible. By the way, this is a very common error."

"This is a good response except R stands for Real numbers and Q stands for rational numbers."

Math Is a Four-Letter Word!

WHAT? Description

This activity asks students to complete the following phrase with a four-letter word: "Math is (a) _____."

Students are then asked to explain their reasoning behind their choice of words. This is a good first-day-of-class assignment as it allows students to express their appreciation or anxiety regarding the learning of algebra. Sharing their metaphors and hearing others make this an illuminating experience.

WHY? Objectives

This activity allows students to:

• Express negative or positive feelings regarding mathematics instruction.

• Lessen anxiety through this self-expression.

• Share and hear others' interpretations of their metaphors.

• Think about mathematics in another way.

• Identify and practice metacognitive skills.

HOW? Examples

Here are some responses that students have made:

"Math is _loud!_ Loud because it keeps me awake at night, trying to solve problems that stumped me."

"Math is _evil_. Math is hard for me. I just don't get it."

"Math is a _rose_. At times it is beautiful, when it just makes sense. But at other times it is full of thorns, and it is so confusing.

Math Is a Four-Letter Word!

NAME _____ DATE _____

±···∞≈∈∞∅±···∞≈∈∞∅±···∅≈∈∞∅±···∈≈∈∞∅±···±≈∈∞∅±···∞≈∈∞∅

Math is _____.

Explanation:

Math is a _____.

Explanation:

E-Writing

±⋯∞≈∈∞∅±⋯∞≈∈∞∅±⋯∞≈∈∞∅±⋯∈≈∈∞∅±⋯±≈∈∞∅±⋯∞≈∈∞∅

WHAT? Description

One of the primary modes of communication today is e-mail. Having students communicate by e-mail gives one more forum for dialogue between student and instructor. This form of messaging is immediate, allowing algebra students to comment on a class as soon as possible or refer to homework problems as they arise. Moreover, if a particular time is set for the instructor to respond to a student's e-mails, then the student and teacher can correspond at the same time.

Students may be asked to send e-mail responses to teacher-generated questions on a regular basis—once a week or every day. The e-messages might be in response to questions about students' progress in the course or questions calling for demonstrating their understanding of content. It is best to give a clear and direct question, such as:

"What did you learn in class today?"

"Summarize the process for finding the slope of a line."

"What was the muddiest point in class today?"

"Write out how you solved the problem on page X from your homework assignment."

"What has been the greatest challenge in this class so far?"

"What has been the easiest concept to understand in this class so far?"

The ground rules for how the teacher expects student responses to look should be given up front—for example: "Use complete sentences, give the correct spelling, and make frequent use of mathematical terms." Teachers are then able to receive feedback before the next class and to correct problems or faulty use of mathematical vocabulary. Students may be encouraged to use new mathematical terms through the awarding of extra points for their correct use.

WHY? Objectives

E-writing allows the algebra student:

- Immediate and direct feedback from the instructor.
- Another forum for communicating algebraically or about algebra.
- Another avenue for voicing concerns or sharing personal problems with the instructor.
- An opportunity to enlarge and use mathematical vocabulary.
- An opportunity to earn credit for work other than exams, quizzes, and homework.
- Time to identify and practice metacognitive skills.

E-writing allows the teacher:

- A forum for dialogue with the student.
- Another medium for assessing student understanding of content.
- An opportunity to correct faulty use of and suggest new mathematical terms.

HOW? Example

The lesson gives an example of a general e-writing assignment.

E-Writing

± ··· ∞ ≈ ∈ ∞ ∅ ± ··· ∞ ≈ ∈ ∞ ∅ ± ··· ∅ ≈ ∈ ∞ ∅ ± ··· ∈ ≈ ∈ ∞ ∅ ± ··· ± ≈ ∈ ∞ ∅ ± ··· ∞ ≈ ∈ ∞ ∅

ASSIGNMENT: Each Friday your e-assignment will be posted on the board. Please respond by Wednesday of the following week. I will be on-line Monday evening from _____ to _____. Feel free to correspond with me at this time.

Each e-mail message must contain the following:

- Write out the weekly e-assignment first.
- Use at least two paragraphs.
- Use complete, clear sentences (remember that writing about mathematics should be concise, uncluttered, and clear).
- Include as many mathematical terms as possible.

You may include other questions about homework or other comments. However, you must also respond to the weekly question using the guidelines above.

Grading:

Each e-mail is worth _____ points.
Extra points will be given for every new mathematical term used correctly after the first two terms.

Algebra Out Loud

Math Similes, Metaphors, and Analogies

$\pm \cdots \infty \approx \in \infty \varnothing \pm \cdots \infty \approx \in \infty \varnothing \pm \cdots \varnothing \approx \in \infty \varnothing \pm \cdots \in \approx \in \infty \varnothing \pm \cdots \pm \approx \in \infty \varnothing \pm \cdots \infty \approx \in \infty \varnothing$

WHAT? Description

Similes, metaphors, and analogies are words and phrases that are used to conjure up vivid word pictures of related concepts. A *simile* is a comparison using the words *like* or *as*—for example, "Set A is like the set of counting numbers." A *metaphor* is a direct comparison suggesting that a concept is a word that quickly brings to mind a related picture—for example, "A prime number is a simple yet important creature." An *analogy* is an enhanced simile or metaphor—for example, "The empty set is a black hole where solutions and questions seem to be sucked up and to disappear into the darkness."

For the following activity, students were asked to reflect on concepts from the day's lesson and create a simile, a metaphor, and an analogy for each term:

Concept	Simile	Metaphor	Analogy
Relation	Like a family member	A relation is a handshake.	A relation is a handshake between friends.
Function	Like a spouse	A function is a marriage of sorts.	A function is a marriage where each spouse has her or his role.
Composition	As socks are to shoes are to the person who wears them	A composition is the relationship of a baby to its grandmother.	A composition is a relationship between a baby and its biological mother and grandmother.

WHY? Objectives

The math similes, metaphors, and analogies activity allows the student to:

- Consider the definition and features of certain math concepts.
- Express math concepts in familiar terms.
- Learn more about math concepts through consideration of comparisons.
- Identify and practice metacognitive skills.

HOW? Examples

The following are examples of this activity.

Math Similes, Metaphors, and Analogies

NAME _____   DATE _____

± ··· ∞ ≈ ∈ ∞ ∅ ± ··· ∞ ≈ ∈ ∞ ∅ ± ··· ∅ ≈ ∈ ∞ ∅ ± ··· ∈ ≈ ∈ ∞ ∅ ± ··· ± ≈ ∈ ∞ ∅ ± ··· ∞ ≈ ∈ ∞ ∅

ASSIGNMENT: Fill in the blank spaces below with an appropriate simile, metaphor, and analogy. Recall that a simile is a comparison using the words *like* or *as*—for example, "A graph is like a road on a map." A *metaphor* is a direct comparison suggesting that a concept is a word that quickly brings to mind a related picture—for example, "Infinity is a bottomless sea." An *analogy* is an enhanced simile or metaphor—for example, "Infinity is a bottomless sea with numbers swimming on forever."

Use comparisons of things or words that you are familiar with. Be creative!

Concept	Simile	Metaphor	Analogy
Line			
Slope			
Intercept			
Parallel			
Perpendicular			

Writing as Authentic Assessment

Math Similes, Metaphors, and Analogies
(continued)

Concept	Simile	Metaphor	Analogy
Algebra			
Equation			
Variable			
Constant			
Coefficient			

Math Similes, Metaphors, and Analogies

(continued)

NAME _____ DATE _____

± ··· ∞ ≈ ∈ ∞ ∅ ± ··· ∞ ≈ ∈ ∞ ∅ ± ··· ∅ ≈ ∈ ∞ ∅ ± ··· ∈ ≈ ∈ ∞ ∅ ± ··· ± ≈ ∈ ∞ ∅ ± ··· ∞ ≈ ∈ ∞ ∅

Concept	Simile	Metaphor	Analogy
Commutative property			
Associative property			
Distributive property			
Closure property			
Identity			
Inverse			

Targeted Problem-Solving Assessments

$\pm \cdots \infty \approx \in \infty \oslash \pm \cdots \infty \approx \in \infty \oslash \pm \cdots \oslash \approx \in \infty \oslash \pm \cdots \in \approx \in \infty \oslash \pm \cdots \pm \approx \in \infty \oslash \pm \cdots \infty \approx \in \infty \oslash$

WHAT? Description

The targeted problem-solving assessment activity allows teachers to assess students' understanding of certain problem-solving processes and make decisions about whether more time should be spent on the targeted content. Teachers design a worksheet with three to five problems of the same type and give the sheet to students. On the worksheet, students are asked to name or describe the problem-solving process they will use on each problem and then solve each problem. This activity causes students to consider which problem-solving technique they should use before they leap into an incorrect process.

This activity is very similar to Angelo and Cross's Documented Problem Solutions (1993). They suggest that this process has two aims: "(1) to assess how students solve problems and (2) to assess how well students understand and can describe their problem-solving methods" (p. 222).

By examining the worksheets, the teacher is able to make decisions about time and coverage of content for this particular class.

WHY? Objectives

Using the targeted problem-solving assessment activity allows teachers to:

- Gauge students' overall understanding and articulation of content.
- Gauge an individual student's understanding and articulation of content.
- Make decisions about time and coverage of content.
- Identify and practice metacognitive skills.

HOW? Examples

The lessons provide examples of this activity.

Targeted Problem-Solving Assessments

NAME _____ DATE _____

$\pm \cdots \infty \approx \in \infty \varnothing \pm \cdots \infty \approx \in \infty \varnothing \pm \cdots \varnothing \approx \in \infty \varnothing \pm \cdots \in \approx \in \infty \varnothing \pm \cdots \pm \approx \in \infty \varnothing \pm \cdots \infty \approx \in \infty \varnothing$

ASSIGNMENT: Read and reflect on each problem. Name or describe the problem-solving process you will use to solve the problem in the space provided. Finally, solve the problem, showing each step clearly and completely. You may use another sheet of paper for this part.

1. Solve $x^3 = 27$.

Name or description of the process to be used: _____

2. Solve $x^4 - 16 = 0$.

Name or description of the process to be used: _____

3. Solve $x^3 - 8 = 0$.

Name or description of the process to be used: _____

4. Solve $x^4 = 81$.

Name or description of the process to be used: _____

Targeted Problem-Solving Assessments

NAME _____   DATE _____

$\pm \cdots \infty \approx \in \infty \varnothing \pm \cdots \infty \approx \in \infty \varnothing \pm \cdots \varnothing \approx \in \infty \varnothing \pm \cdots \in \approx \in \infty \varnothing \pm \cdots \pm \approx \in \infty \varnothing \pm \cdots \infty \approx \in \infty \varnothing$

ASSIGNMENT: Read and reflect on each problem. Name or describe the problem-solving process you will use to solve the problem in the space provided. Finally, solve the problem, showing each step clearly and completely. You may use another sheet of paper for this part.

1. Graph in the xy plane: $2x - 4y = 12$

Name or description of the process to be used: _____

2. Graph in the xy plane: $y = 5x + 8$

Name or description of the process to be used: _____

3. Graph in the xy plane: $3y = -8$

Name or description of the process to be used: _____

4. Graph in the xy plane: $x = 4$

Name or description of the process to be used: _____

Algebra Out Loud

Targeted Problem-Solving Assessments

NAME _____   DATE _____

ASSIGNMENT: Read and reflect on each problem. Name or describe the problem-solving process you will use to solve the problem. Finally, solve the problem, showing each step clearly and completely. You may use another sheet of paper for this part.

1. Simplify: $(x^3)^0$

Name or description of the process to be used: _____

2. Simplify: $\dfrac{x^{-9}}{x^{-2}}$

Name or description of the process to be used: _____

3. Simplify: $x^{-5}(x^4)(x^{-3})$

Name or description of the process to be used: _____

4. Simplify: $(a^5)^{-2}$

Name or description of the process to be used: _____

Self-Portrait as a Learner of Algebra

WHAT? Description

This activity asks students to paint a verbal portrait of themselves as a learner of algebra. Questions are written in such a way that they elicit descriptive responses from the student responder. Students who are artistically inclined may decide to sketch themselves as learners of algebra. Students whose interests lie elsewhere are invited to use those interests to describe themselves as a learner of anything.

WHY? Objectives

The completion of a self-portrait as a learner of algebra allows the student to:

- Identify and practice metacognitive skills.
- Consider and document his or her algebraic skills and talents.
- Gauge progress as a learner of algebra.

HOW? Example

See the lesson that follows for a sample questionnaire.

Self-Portrait as a Learner of Algebra

NAME _____ DATE _____

Part One: Type of Learner

I best learn algebra when I can _____

_____

I best learn algebra when the teacher _____

_____

Part Two: Description of Learner in Math Terms

Which of the following descriptors (math terms) best describe you as a learner of algebra? Check all that apply.

Maximum _____   Variable _____   Linear _____

Minimum _____   Constant _____   Parabolic _____

Infinite _____   Exponential _____   Cubical _____

Finite _____   Divisible _____   Spherical _____

Self-Portrait as a Learner of Algebra (continued)

NAME _____   DATE _____

$\pm \cdots \infty \approx \in \infty \varnothing \pm \cdots \infty \approx \in \infty \varnothing \pm \cdots \varnothing \approx \in \infty \varnothing \pm \cdots \in \approx \in \infty \varnothing \pm \cdots \pm \approx \in \infty \varnothing \pm \cdots \infty \approx \in \infty \varnothing$

Part Three: Interest/Knowledge/Skills of Learner*

Rate your interest in, skills concerning, and knowledge of the following algebra topics, using the chart below. Use the following key:

0 = No interest   N = No skills, no knowledge
1 = Some interest   B = Basic skills and knowledge
2 = Interested in learning more   H = Can do it and know about it adequately
3 = Very interested   W = Can do it well and know a lot about it

	INTEREST				SKILLS/KNOWLEDGE			
Factoring trinomials	0	1	2	3	N	B	H	W
Solving simple linear equations	0	1	2	3	N	B	H	W
Recognizing functions	0	1	2	3	N	B	H	W
Graphing linear functions	0	1	2	3	N	B	H	W
Solving quadratic equations, one variable	0	1	2	3	N	B	H	W
Graphing quadratic functions	0	1	2	3	N	B	H	W

Part Four: Self-Portrait of Learner

Create a portrait of yourself as a learner of algebra. Your portrait may be a drawing, a verbal description, a poem, a quantitative summary, or any other form that you feel adequately displays you as an algebraist or a student of algebra. Use the back of this page or a sheet of graph paper.

-----

*Part Three is adapted from Angelo and Cross (1993).

$$\pm \cdots \infty \approx \in \infty \varnothing \pm \cdots \varnothing \approx \in \infty \varnothing$$

Writing for Assessment

Prelude

The Assessment Principle from the NCTM's Principles and Standards for School Mathematics (2000) states:

"Assessment should support the learning of important mathematics and furnish useful information to both teachers and students. . . . Assessment should not be done to students; rather, it should be done for students. . . . Assessment should become a routine part of the ongoing classroom activity rather than an interruption . . . assembling evidence from a variety of sources is more likely to yield an accurate picture" (pp. 22–24).

In other words, assessment should be part of the learning process for both student and teacher, not merely a traffic light directing students to stop or go onward and upward. Writing for assessment is one mode of evaluation that supports the NCTM's recommendations. Students demonstrate their understanding of mathematical concepts through their writings, and teachers give valuable feedback or add to the students' written understanding by their responses.

The activities in this chapter are meant to be read and graded by the teacher. These activities should be assigned early in the course and throughout the entire course. Students' communication skills usually improve with practice. Also, writing for assessment is considered a writing strategy or a larger category of writing strategies by many writers.

Angelo and Cross (1993) suggest that for quality instruction, "faculty must first classify exactly what they want students in their courses to learn" (p. 13). In an algebra course, there is usually a list of more than fifty concepts teachers want their students to know. Perhaps ten of these concepts are important enough that teachers would want students to be able to understand and explain these concepts ten years from now. It is these concepts that writing-for-assessment activities could effectively target. For example, solving simple linear equations is a very useful process that unites critical and logical thinking with the notion of generalization and a process that students may very well use again. Writing about this process helps solidify the process and applications of the process.

This chapter contains the following activities along with several lessons:

Math portfolios

Math essays

Write questions

Math posters

In addition, many of the activities presented in Chapter Five could fall into the writing for assessment category, just as many of the activities in this chapter could fall into the writing-to-understand-algebra category.

Math Portfolios

WHAT? Description

A portfolio is a dossier or a collection of materials that is representative of a person's work. A student's math portfolio may contain writing assignments, exams, notes, or homework. Ideally, the portfolio contains papers that demonstrate the student's progress in a single mathematics course or for all mathematics courses taken in high school or when earning a college degree.

Students might be asked to keep all writing-to-learn-mathematics papers along with other more traditional assignments. Eventually, the student chooses either the best pieces or the pieces that demonstrate growth or progress for the dossier. The student should append written reactions to the chosen pieces and, perhaps, to the entire portfolio. Guidelines for the contents of the portfolio and assessment criteria should be given to the students. A checklist may be used for assessing the portfolio. Presenting students with a checklist for the assessment of the portfolio may assist them in their choices for and creation of the portfolio.

WHY? Objectives

The math portfolio gives the student the opportunity to:

- Demonstrate progress in a mathematics course or over several courses.
- Review and reflect on the mathematics learned.
- See personal growth in mathematical understanding.

The math portfolio gives the teacher the opportunity to:

- Assess an individual student's progress in a mathematics course or over several courses.
- Gauge student comprehension and revise courses appropriately.

HOW? Suggestions

Following are some suggestions for pieces to be included in a math portfolio:

- An introductory essay detailing the writer's vision of the portfolio
- Contents page
- All notes from one chapter
- Ten homework assignments with written reactions
- All writing-to-learn-mathematics activities, such as MOs, ads, poems, graph descriptions, and letters
- At least two exams or quizzes that demonstrate improvement, along with a statement detailing this progress
- Math autobiography
- Philosophy of learning mathematics
- A conclusion that describes or sums up the writer's mathematical experience in this course

Math Portfolios

NAME _____   DATE _____

± ⋯ ∞ ≈ ∈ ∞ ∅ ± ⋯ ∞ ≈ ∈ ∞ ∅ ± ⋯ ∅ ≈ ∈ ∞ ∅ ± ⋯ ∈ ≈ ∈ ∞ ∅ ± ⋯ ± ≈ ∈ ∞ ∅ ± ⋯ ∞ ≈ ∈ ∞ ∅

ASSIGNMENT: Keep all writing-in-mathematics pieces, notes, homework assignments, and exams in a dossier or binder. Eventually, you will be asked to choose your best pieces from this collection for a math portfolio. Your portfolio must contain at least the following items:

- A cover sheet and a table of contents
- All notes for one chapter of your choosing
- Ten hand-in homework assignments with your written reactions to your work attached to each
- All writings composed for this course
- At least two exams or quizzes that demonstrate improvement, with a statement detailing this progress
- A concluding essay that describes your mathematics experience in this course

Portfolio Assessment Checklist

	Yes	No	Points
1. The portfolio contains all of the pieces listed:	____	____	____/40
Cover sheet with table of contents	____	____	
All notes for one chapter	____	____	
Ten hand-in homework assignments	____	____	
All writings from this course	____	____	
Two exams or quizzes	____	____	
Concluding essay	____	____	
2. Homework assignments have satisfactory written reactions attached.	____	____	____/10
3. Exams have clear statements that demonstrate progress.	____	____	____/10
4. Concluding essay is clearly written and adequately describes the student's mathematical experience.	____	____	____/20
5. Overall appearance of the portfolio is neat and easy to follow.	____	____	____/10
6. The portfolio is creative and clearly shows the personality of the student creator.	____	____	____/10

TOTAL POINTS EARNED   ____/100

COMMENTS:

Math Portfolios: Algebra

NAME _____ DATE _____

± ···∞ ≈ ∈ ∞ ⌀ ± ···∞ ≈ ∈ ∞ ⌀ ± ··· ⌀ ≈ ∈ ∞ ⌀ ± ···∈ ≈ ∈ ∞ ⌀ ± ··· ± ≈ ∈ ∞ ⌀ ± ···∞ ≈ ∈ ∞ ⌀

ASSIGNMENT: Keep all writing-in-mathematics pieces, notes, homework assignments, and exams from your algebra courses in a dossier or binder. Eventually, you will be asked to choose your best pieces from this collection for a math portfolio. Your portfolio must contain at least the following:

- A cover sheet and a table of contents
- At least one piece of work on your favorite topic in algebra
- Several hand-in homework assignments that show your progress in understanding algebra; attach a written reaction to each
- All writings composed for algebra courses
- At least two exams or quizzes that demonstrate improvement, with a statement detailing this progress
- A concluding essay that describes your mathematics experience with algebra

Portfolio Assessment Checklist

	Yes	No	Points
1. The portfolio contains all of the pieces listed:	____	____	____/40
Cover sheet with table of contents	____	____	
At least one favorite	____	____	
Hand-in homework assignments	____	____	
All writings from this course	____	____	
Two exams or quizzes	____	____	
Concluding essay	____	____	
2. Homework assignments have satisfactory written reactions attached.	____	____	____/10
3. Exams have clear statements that demonstrate progress.	____	____	____/10
4. Concluding essay is clearly written and adequately describes the student's mathematical experience.	____	____	____/20
5. Overall appearance of the portfolio is neat and easy to follow.	____	____	____/10
6. The portfolio is creative and clearly shows the personality of the student creator.	____	____	____/10

TOTAL POINTS EARNED   ____/100

COMMENTS:

Math Essays

± … ∞ ≈ ∈ ∞ ∅ ± … ∞ ≈ ∈ ∞ ∅ ± … ∅ ≈ ∈ ∞ ∅ ± … ∈ ≈ ∈ ∞ ∅ ± … ± ≈ ∈ ∞ ∅ ± … ∞ ≈ ∈ ∞ ∅

WHAT? Description

One of the more common writing assignments for secondary and college students in disciplines other than mathematics is the essay. Essay writing can be a powerful assessment tool for both the mathematics teacher and student. The writing of an essay requires many of the same skills that mathematical problem solving requires. Essays should be well thought out and well organized in a clear, step-by-step format.

An essay is a short literary composition written to demonstrate the personal view of the writer. The five-paragraph essay provides a simple format for the student to follow and a good forum in which to display his or her opinion or thesis. The first paragraph introduces the thesis, the middle three paragraphs form the body of the essay and the supporting argument of the thesis, and the last paragraph contains the conclusion or summary of the essay.

The best math essays stem from well-written essay questions. Good essay questions present the topic and pose related questions. Students need to know exactly what the teacher expects in terms of the topic and format of the essay. Are grammar and spelling as important as the content and argument for the thesis? Should the writer consider the teacher as the only audience? Is the essay to be typed or hand written? What does an A essay look like? A grading rubric and a sample of an A paper may be shared with students to assist their efforts in composing a quality math essay.

The algebra instructor might assign a writing project on some topic in the history of algebra or on an application of algebra in today's world. In *Writing with a Purpose,* Trimmer (1995) suggests having the student answer several questions regarding determining her or his purpose of the writing project. The following questions, similar to Trimmer's, are adapted to the unique assignment of writing with purpose about a mathematics topic:

- What are the requirements regarding this assignment? How much mathematics should be included?
- What do I need to know about my topic? What sources will I get the information from? Do I know enough about the topic to get started right away?

- What will my hypothesis be? (Recall that a hypothesis is an unproven theory or supposition.) How many other hypotheses exist? Does my choice in hypotheses make sense?

- What purpose have I discovered for my writing project? Has it changed as I researched my topic?

- What is my thesis? Does it make a clear, well-defined, and well-detailed summary about what my writing intends to do? Does it necessarily follow from my working hypothesis?

WHY? Objectives

Composing a math essay gives the student the opportunity to:

- Research and reflect on a key mathematical concept.
- Clarify and present his or her view and understanding of the topic.
- Practice writing and communication skills.

The reading of students' math essays allows the teacher to:

- Assess students' understanding of concepts.
- Respond to students' misconceptions.
- Praise students' efforts.
- See the topic through the words of the student essayist.

HOW? Examples

Two examples of good essay questions follow in the lessons.

Math Essays: Quadratic Function

NAME _____ DATE _____

± ··∞≈ ∈∞∅ ± ··∞≈ ∈∞∅ ± ··∅≈ ∈∞∅ ± ··∈ ≈ ∈∞∅ ± ··± ≈ ∈∞∅ ± ··∞≈ ∈∞∅

ASSIGNMENT: Compose a well-organized essay describing how to graph a quadratic function without using any graphing technology. Use the five-paragraph format and address the following questions in your essay:

- What shape does the graph take? How do the coefficients or constants in the function affect this shape?

- Extrema are the maxima or minima of a function. What determines the extrema of a quadratic function?

- How are the intercepts of a quadratic found? What significance do they have?

- Should students be allowed to use a graphing calculator to graph quadratics when they first learn about them? If not then, when?

Grading Rubric

- The format is worth 20%. The first paragraph should introduce your thesis. The next three paragraphs should comprise your support of your thesis. The last paragraph should be the conclusion and should tie it all together.

- The accuracy of the facts and the substance and thoroughness of your argument for your thesis are worth 60%. This includes the answers to the questions posed above.

- Clarity and mechanics are worth 20%. Your essay must be word-processed and spell-checked. Complete sentences are expected.

Grading Sheet

Points   **Comments**

Format: _____ (20%)

Content: _____ (60%)

Clarity and mechanics: _____ (20%)

Total grade: _____

Math Essays: Using a Graphing Calculator in Algebra

NAME _____ DATE _____

ASSIGNMENT: In a well-organized essay, write about how the graphing calculator assists in learning algebra. Be sure to answer the following questions in your essay:

- Some people believe using a calculator is cheating. When is it? When is it not?
- What features have you learned about directly from using your calculator? How has the calculator enhanced or diminished your understanding of mathematics?
- How are calculators used in the work world?

Grading Rubric

- The format is worth 20%. The first paragraph should introduce your thesis. The next three paragraphs should comprise your support of your thesis. The last paragraph should be the conclusion and should tie it all together.
- The accuracy of the facts and the substance and thoroughness of your argument for your thesis are worth 60%. This includes the answers to the questions posed above.
- Clarity and mechanics are worth 20%. Your essay must be word-processed and spell-checked. Complete sentences are expected.

Grading Sheet

Points   **Comments**

Format: _____ (20%)

Content: _____ (60%)

Clarity and mechanics: _____ (20%)

Total grade: _____

Copyright © 2003 by John Wiley & Sons, Inc.

Math Essays: Algebra, the Real World, and Me

NAME _____   DATE _____

$+ \cdots \infty \approx \in \infty \varnothing \pm \cdots \infty \approx \in \infty \varnothing \pm \cdots \varnothing \approx \in \infty \varnothing \pm \cdots \in \approx \in \infty \varnothing \pm \cdots \pm \approx \in \infty \varnothing \pm \cdots \infty \approx \in \infty \varnothing$

ASSIGNMENT: Compose a clear and well-organized essay on the usefulness of algebra in the real world. State your opinion and defend it. Be sure to address the following issues:

- Algebra is abstract and gives generalizations of particular types of problems.
- Certain learners prefer algebra over finite mathematics courses that include many applications.
- Understanding algebra reinforces critical-thinking skills and problem solving in general.

Grading Rubric

- The format is worth 20%. The first paragraph should introduce your thesis. The next three paragraphs should comprise your support of your thesis. The last paragraph should be the conclusion and should tie it all together.
- The accuracy of the facts and the substance and thoroughness of your argument for your thesis are worth 60%. This includes the answers to the questions posed above.
- Clarity and mechanics are worth 20%. Your essay must be word-processed and spell-checked. Complete sentences are expected.

Grading Sheet

Points   **Comments**

Format: _____ (20%)

Content: _____ (60%)

Clarity and mechanics: _____ (20%)

Total grade: _____

Write Questions

WHAT? Description

Write questions are questions that require the mathematics student to respond in writing rather than merely use computation. Write questions are used in hand-in homework, quizzes, and exams. When using write questions as part of quizzes or exams, it is a good idea to introduce this type of question to the student as a part of homework. Students need time to practice writing and to consider how writing about mathematics compares to other writing.

Write questions should require a short answer, usually two to three sentences. Students should be expected to give answers in paragraph form, the form that they probably will be expected to use in their future careers. The questions themselves usually begin in the following ways:

Describe . . .

Write out the definition in your own words of . . .

Write out the method for . . .

Compare or contrast . . .

WHY? Objectives

Write questions allow the student writer to:

- Practice communicating mathematically.
- Demonstrate how he or she understands algebra.
- Consider the features and fine points regarding an algebraic concept.

Write questions allow the teacher to:

- Assess student understanding of algebraic concepts.
- Observe and appreciate the various ways that students understand algebra.

HOW? Examples

The following list gives examples of write questions that may be used in algebra assignments or exams:

- Describe how the local maximum of a polynomial function is found using a graphing calculator. Use at least three complete and clear sentences in paragraph form.
- Write out the definition for a function in your own words in paragraph form.
- Write out the method for completing the square in paragraph form.
- Compare and contrast point slope form and slope intercept form of a linear equation. Use at least three complete and clear sentences in paragraph form.
- Give an application for a quadratic equation and explain how the equation can be used to solve this application. Use at least three sentences in paragraph form.

Write Questions: Write Question of the Day

NAME _____   DATE _____

±⋯∞≈∈∞∅±⋯∞≈∈∞∅±⋯∅≈∈∞∅±⋯∈≈∈∞∅±⋯±≈∈∞∅±⋯∞≈∈∞∅

ASSIGNMENT: The write questions are designed to help you explore and further understand the math concepts discussed in class. Often these questions do not have a right or wrong answer; rather, they require you to take a stand.

Each question of the day is worth 5 points, and there is a total of 50 possible points to earn. You are required to respond to 10 write questions over the semester but may turn in more. Your lowest scores will be dropped if you elect to turn in more than ten write questions.

Each response must include at least three complete sentences of explanation. Examples, graphs, and pictures are also allowed and encouraged. The point is: Make your answer clear! It may help to imagine you are explaining it to another student.

Responses will be graded on accuracy, clarity, and creativity. Clarity includes correct grammar and vocabulary.

Write Question

Which do you believe is larger: the set of natural numbers or the set of integers? Justify or defend your answer.

Here are some examples of students' responses to several write questions:

1. Describe how to solve the linear equation: $ax + b = 0$. Assume a and b are positive integers.

Student answer: "$ax + b = 0$ can be written $h(x) = ax + b$ so you could use the x intercept method to solve. Put the equation on a graph and find the point where x intercepts the x-axis. The 'x' coordinate of that point needs to be plugged into the equation and it should equal zero. That x point is the solution."

Teacher response: "Excellent explanation of the use of the x intercept graphing method of solving a linear equation in one variable. . . . Is this the method you would use for solving $2x + 4 = 0$?"

2. Compare and contrast the similarities and differences between solving a linear equation and a linear inequality.

Student answer: "A difference between the two [equations] is that with an inequality, the function is not set equal to another number, but to a value that is greater than or equal to the answer. A similarity is that you can solve both [equations] by adding, subtracting, dividing, and multiplying. The only difference is that with an inequality the sign (greater or less than) changes when dividing or multiplying by a negative number."

Teacher response: The writer accurately identified a major distinction between the solving of an equation and inequality . . . . "dividing or multiplying by a negative number" causes the inequality sign to change direction. However, the writer refers to both inequality and equation as "equations," which is inaccurate, as I pointed out. Algebra students often struggle with learning and using the correct terms and notation. This is an example where it was addressed before testing.

Another student answer: "Both can be solved symbolically, numerically, and graphically. . . . When you solve it's important to note only equations have equal signs, so only they can be set equal to zero. The solutions to inequalities can be found by setting two of them equal to each other, as opposed to 0."

Teacher response: "Your last sentence is unclear. I assume you were implying that you would use the graphing method to solve an inequality? One major difference between solving inequalities and solving equations (algebraically) is that when multiplying or dividing an inequality by a negative value, you must switch the direction of the inequality sign."

3. **Discuss the relationship between the slope formula and the point-slope form of a linear equation.**

Student answer: "The slope formula is used in algebra to find the slope of a line. Point slope formula is used to find the equation of a line when you have certain conditions. Ex. Slope = 2.4 passing through (4,5). The relation between the two could be best described by examples:

Slope formula $\quad\quad\quad m = \dfrac{y_2 - y_1}{x_2 - x_1}$

Point slope $\quad\quad\quad\quad y_2 - y_1 = m\,(x_2 - x_1)$

"And when you cross-multiply the point slope formula, your result will be $m = \dfrac{y_2 - y_1}{x_2 - x_1}$. So you have a direct relationship between the slope form [formula] and point slope form of a linear equation."

Teacher response: Again we see the struggle with the correct term to use "slope form," which should be *slope formula*. However, this student clearly understands the development from the slope to the point slope form, although he did express it as a "direct relationship," which is a little unclear. Students also struggle with when it is okay to drop the subscripts and the idea that "x" and "y" could be substituted into the point slope formula for x_2 and y_2 without loss of generalization.

4. **It has been said that piecewise-defined functions often serve as better models for real-life situations than other continuous functions such as linear or quadratic functions. Explain why.**

Student answer: "Piecewise-defined functions often serve as better models for real-life situations than other continuous functions such as linear or quadratic functions because in real-life situations it is possible that no single formula can conveniently represent f. Because piecewise-defined functions typically use different formulas on various intervals of the domain, they are therefore better to serve as models for real-life situations."

Another student answer: "Piece-wise functions are best for real-life situations because it rarely happens that 'f' is the same always. The book used the example of postage costs. If you mail a letter weighing an ounce or less you pay one price. If your piece of mail weighs over one ounce but less than two, you'll have to pay a different price, etc."

Teacher response to second student: "I agree real-life functions are not always neat. Look at the greatest integer function on page xx for another look at postage costs."

Algebra Out Loud

5. **The midpoint formula is used to find the midpoint between two points in the *xy* plane. How can this formula be adapted to find the midpoint between two points on a ruler?**

Student answer: "The midpoint on a ruler can be found by solving the formula. You need to pick the two points you want to solve from the ruler. Solve the two points like you would any midpoint formula problem."

Teacher response: "The midpoint formula is $\left(\frac{x_1 + x_2}{2}, \frac{y_1 + y_2}{2} \right)$. Two points on a ruler would have only two values, not two ordered pairs (x,y). Explain how you would adapt this formula."

The following example of write question also illustrates how student understanding of concepts was unveiled:

6. **How does the discriminant tell us how many and what type of solutions a quadratic equation will have?**

Student answer: "The discriminant tells us how many and what type of solutions a quadratic equation will have by looking at its sign. If the discriminant is less than 0, there will be no solution, this is because you cannot take the square root of a negative number. If the discriminant is greater than 0, there will be two real solutions. And if the discriminant is equal to 0, there will be one real solution.

"Discriminant $\rightarrow b^2 - 4ac$"

Teacher response: We had not yet discussed imaginary solutions in this course, so this student's response was good. Many students copied the rules from the text, and I was unsure that they understood the concept of discriminant. Therefore, the day after I graded their responses, I gave a quiz to assess this knowledge. The students who copied the rules from the book scored poorly and those who wrote their own (as the student above did) did well.

Math Posters

WHAT? Description

In a recent History of Mathematics course, college students and future mathematics teachers were assigned the creation of a poster to complement the biographies they were writing. Each student chose a famous mathematician, researched and wrote a biography of this person, and created a math poster as a visual aid for their fifteen-minute presentation of their work. Of course, math posters can be created using any mathematical concept, any person involved with mathematics, or any place where mathematics is created or used as the poster's theme. The posters can grace bulletin boards and be used in future lessons.

In the college course, each student gave a personal touch to her or his poster. The completed posters were laminated as most of the students planned to use their posters in their future classrooms.

WHY? Objectives

The creation of math posters caused the students to:

- Consider the significant attributes or contributions of their personas.
- Add something of themselves to the biographical information of their papers.
- Appreciate and learn from the posters of their peers.
- Consider how the poster will facilitate and complement their future instruction.

HOW? Examples

See the next few pages for examples of an assignment sheet and student posters.

Biography of Mathematician Poster Presentation

$\pm\cdots\infty\approx\in\infty\varnothing\pm\cdots\infty\approx\in\infty\varnothing\pm\cdots\varnothing\approx\in\infty\varnothing\pm\cdots\in\approx\in\infty\varnothing\pm\cdots\pm\approx\in\infty\varnothing\pm\cdots\infty\approx\in\infty\varnothing$

ASSIGNMENT:

WRITE-UP

You are to compose a 3- to 5-page word-processed biography of the mathematician assigned to you. (See topic assignment sheet.) The write-up must contain the following components:

- Early life
- Education and life's work
- Mathematical contributions
- Later life
- A time line of important dates

It may be difficult to find information for each category for your mathematician, so use what you can find.

POSTER

The assignment is to fill a poster with images and writings that illustrate your mathematician. Use a large sheet of poster board for the background and copies of pictures, examples of math work, or schematics that represent your mathematician for the poster content. You may choose to include your time line on the poster. Your objective is to allow us to "see" or get to know your subject. Be creative.

RESOURCES

Use at least four different sources with at least one from the library. Use a consistent format for citing resources and include a bibliography page.

PRESENTATION

10- to 15-minute demonstration and exploration of your poster subject.

GRADING

Accuracy	10 points	(content and math work)
Clarity and mechanics	10	(writing, grammar, vocabulary, spelling)
Creativity and insight	10	
Resources	10	(at least four cited references)
Presentation	10	
Total	50 points	

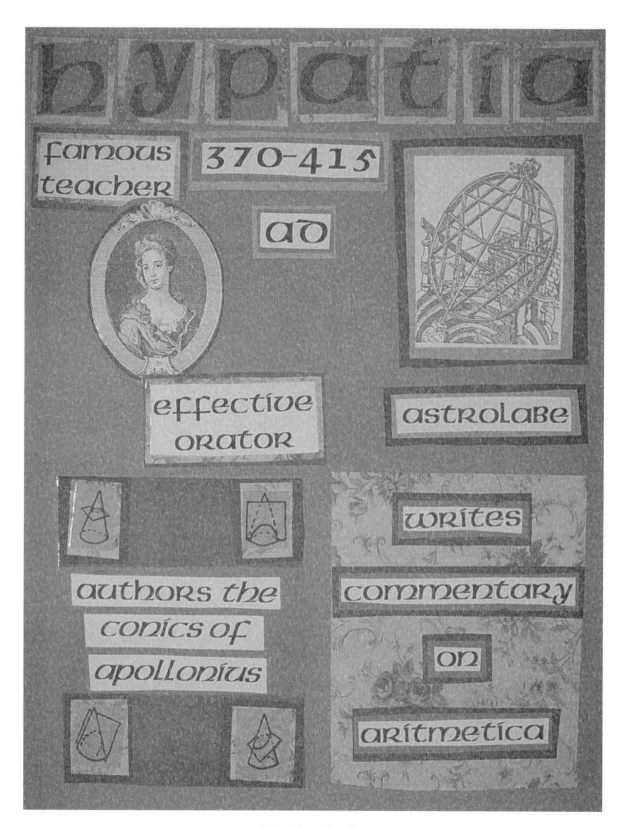

hypatia

famous teacher

370-415 ad

effective orator

astrolabe

writes

commentary

on

authors the conics of apollonius

aritmetica

By Jo Marie Rozelle

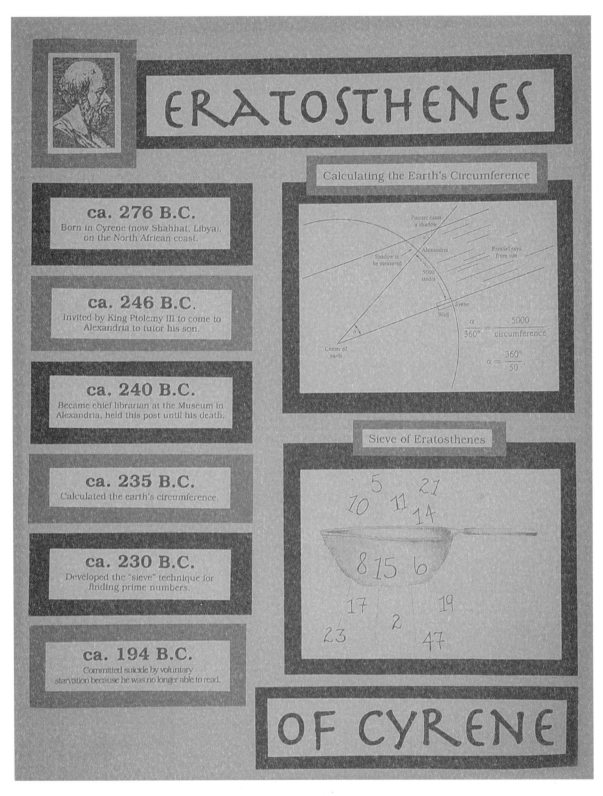

By Mary Feltner

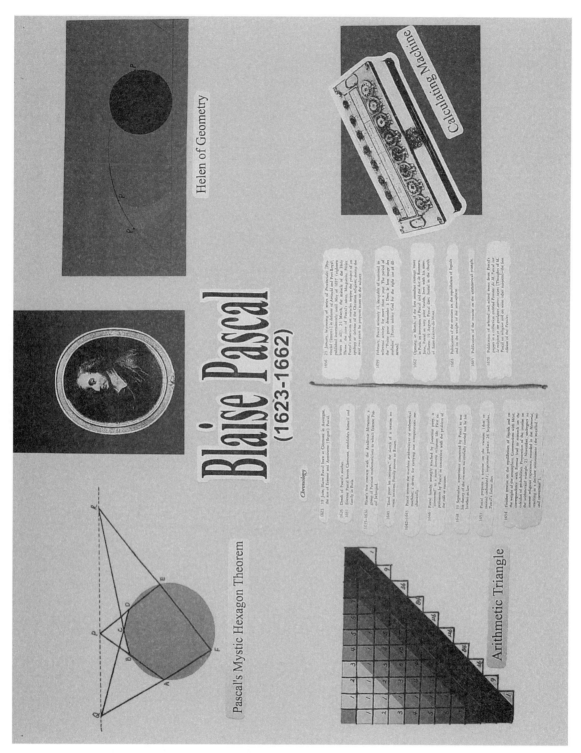

Helen of Geometry

Calculating Machine

Blaise Pascal
(1623-1662)

Pascal's Mystic Hexagon Theorem

Arithmetic Triangle

By Inshin Kim

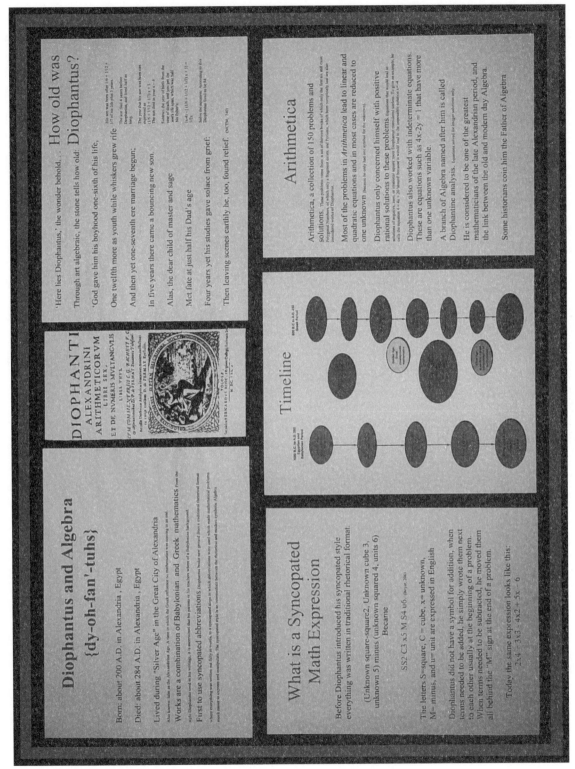

By David Sloop

By Fred Hollinghead

Algebra Out Loud

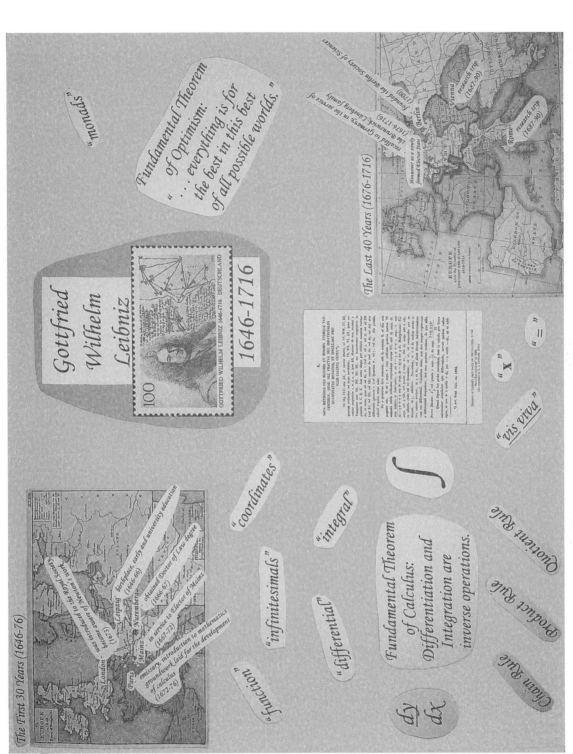

"monads"

Fundamental Theorem of Optimism: ". . . everything is for the best in this best of all possible worlds."

Founded the Berlin Society of Sciences (1700)

Vienna research trip (1687-90)

Rome research trip (1687-90)

Traveled to Germany in the service of the Brunswick-Lüneburg family (1676-1716)

Hannover as a newly formed Elector State

The Last 40 Years (1676-1716)

EUROPE

Gottfried Wilhelm Leibniz

GOTTFRIED WILHELM LEIBNIZ 1646-1716 DEUTSCHLAND

100

1646-1716

"x"

"="

"vis viva"

∫

"coordinates"

"integral"

Quotient Rule

Product Rule

Chain Rule

"infinitesimals"

"differential"

Fundamental Theorem of Calculus: Differentiation and Integration are inverse operations.

$\frac{dy}{dx}$

"function"

The First 30 Years (1646-76)

EUROPE

Leipzig: birthplace, early and university education (1646-66)

obtained Doctor of Law Degree (1666-67)

was introduced to the 1670s Society (1673)

Mainz/Nuremberg: in service to Elector of Mainz (1667-72)

Paris: emissary; introduction to mathematics; groundwork laid for the development of calculus (1672-76)

London

By Jenny Banks

References

Angelo, T. A., and Cross, P. K. *Classroom Assessment Techniques: A Handbook for College Teachers.* (2nd ed.) San Francisco: Jossey-Bass, 1993.

Baldwin, R. S., Ford, J. C., and Readance, J. E. "Teaching Word Connotations: An Alternative Strategy." *Reading World,* 1981, *21,* 103–108.

Barron, R. F. "The Use of Vocabulary as Advance Organizer." In H. L. Herber and P. L. Sanders (eds.), *Research in Reading in the Content Areas: First Report.* Syracuse, N.Y.: Syracuse University Reading and Language Arts Center, 1969.

Billmeyer, R., and Barton, M. L. *Teaching Reading in the Content Areas: If Not Me, Then Who?* (2nd ed.) Aurora, Colo.: McREL, 1998.

Blachowicz, C. "Making Connections: Alternatives to the Vocabulary Notebook." *Journal of Reading,* 1986, *29,* 643–649.

Borasi, R., and Siegel, M. "Reading to Learn Mathematics: New Connections, New Questions, New Challenges." *For the Learning of Mathematics,* 1990, *10,* 9–16.

Burton, D. M. *The History of Mathematics: An Introduction.* (5th ed.) New York: McGraw-Hill.

Fleury, A. "Guided Poetry." Presentation at Washburn University, 2000.

Frayer, D. A., Frederick, W. C., and Klausmeier, H. J. *A Schema for Testing the Level of Concept Mastery.* Madison: University of Wisconsin Research and Development Center for Cognitive Learning, 1969.

Herber, H. *Teaching Reading in Content Areas.* (2nd ed.) Englewood Cliffs, N.J.: Prentice Hall, 1978.

Katz, V. *A History of Mathematics, an Introduction.* (2nd ed.) Reading, Mass.: Addison-Wesley, 1998.

Kiniry, M., and Rose, M. *Critical Strategies for Academic Writing.* Boston: Bedford Books, 1990.

Langer, J. A. "From Theory to Practice: A Rereading Plan." *Journal of Reading,* 1981, *25,* 152–156.

MacBeth, S. J., Harris, E. M, Helmlich, J., and Newsome, C. "Writing to Learn and Learning to Write in Mathematics at Virginia Tech." Presented at the Second International Writing Across the Curriculum Conference, Charleston, S.C., Feb. 1997.

Mower, P. "Writing to Learn College Algebra." Unpublished doctoral dissertation, University of North Dakota, 1995.

Nasar, S. *A Beautiful Mind.* New York: Simon & Schuster, 1998.

National Council of Supervisors of Mathematics. *Essential Mathematics for the 21st Century.* Minneapolis, Minn.: Mathematics Task Force, 1988.

National Council of Teachers of Mathematics. *Principles and Standards for School Mathematics.* Reston, Va.: National Council of Teachers of Mathematics, 2000.

Ogle, D. M. "The Know, Want to Know, Learning Strategy." In K. D. Muth (ed.), *Children's Comprehension of Text.* Newark, Del.: International Reading Association, 1986.

Polya, G. *How to Solve It.* (2nd ed.) Princeton, N.J.: Princeton University Press, 1973. (Original work published in 1945)

Raphael, T. E. "Teaching Question-Answer Relationships, Revisited." *Reading Teacher,* 1986, *39,* 516–522.

Trimmer, J. F. *Writing with a Purpose.* (11th ed.) Boston: Houghton Mifflin, 1995.

Vacca, R. T., and Vacca, J. L. *Content Area Reading.* (6th ed.) Reading, Mass.: Addison-Wesley, 1999.